Cover: Diorama of the siege of Mobile located at the partially reconstructed French Fort Conde, renamed by the British Fort Charlotte, in downtown Mobile, Alabama, now a museum and welcome center.

Sidney Henson Schell is the author of Fort Powell and the Civil War Western Approaches to Mobile Bay 1861-1865.

The Continental Navy on the Gulf Coast 1775-1781: The USS West Florida at the Siege of Mobile 1780

Sidney Henson Schell

Copyright © 2014 Sidney H. Schell

All rights reserved

To Roxie, the adventure continues

Table of Contents

Introduction 6

British West Florida 10

The Colonies Revolt 14

The Willing Raid 17

Oliver Pollock – The New Orleans Connection 29

The Morris 33

Captain William Pickles 35

Spain Declares War Against Britain 37

The British Naval Situation in West Florida 50

HMS Sloop West Florida 53

The Spanish Naval Situation 62

The Battle on Lake Pontchartrain 66

Cruising the Lake 83

The Continental Sloop West Florida at Mobile 88

Sold out of Service 104

Captain Pickles and the Packet Mercury 106

The Spanish Replica 111

Was the Galveston the West Florida 115

    Researching 115

Conclusion 130

Continental Sloop *Hannah*

Revolutionary war schooner similar to the *West Florida*

Introduction

This is a story of small ships and their crews risking their lives for King and country in the frontier back country of Alabama and Mississippi during the Revolutionary war. They fought their battles far from the eyes of the Boston and Philadelphia newspapers. If a Captain of a Continental vessel had sailed from the Chesapeake in 1779, sought out a single ship combat and defeated a much more heavily armed British naval vessel and then succeeded in bringing both back to port the Captain would have been hailed as a hero. A monument to him probably would still be standing in his home town.

Captain William Pickles fought and won such a battle. Pickles' battle was fought on far away Lake Pontchartrain on the boundary between British West Florida and Spanish Louisiana. An insignificant battle in the Revolutionary War big picture scheme of things but tactically it ended British control of Lake Pontchartrain and British access to the Mississippi River from Mississippi Sound. The story leading up to the battle, the difficulty in providing ships and arming such in Spanish New Orleans is intriguing. Captain Pickles fought two battles on the Gulf Coast, the first on Lake Pontchartrain in 1779 and the second as a participant in the siege of Mobile in 1780.

Captain Pickles' vessel was the only Continental military unit that saw active service and fought a battle on the Gulf

Coast during the Revolutionary war. There were privateers active in the Gulf of Mexico and there were individual patriots attached to the Spanish army. Captain James Willing and his volunteers raided the Natchez district and Willing is reputed to have passed through Mobile on his way to and from the Tensaw community.[1] Some seagoing members of Willing's party, who may or may not have been part of a regular Continental military unit, raided in Mobile Bay and carried away a British merchant vessel.

Captain Pickles and the sloop *West Florida* is then Alabama's only direct connection to any Continental military unit during the Revolutionary War. That fact is not found in any previous local histories. In July 2013 I gave a talk on the subject to the General Galvez Chapter of Sons of the American Revolution (a Mobile/Baldwin County, Alabama group). In opening I asked the group for a show of hands if any of them was aware that a commissioned Continental naval vessel took part in the siege of Mobile in 1780. Not a hand was raised.

This is one of those subjects, where, at least from the author's perspective, the details of the research are of nearly equal interest as the subject matter. My first draft was written in 1976 but there were questions remaining that took the nearly 40 intervening years of occasional research to resolve. The history and the course of the research leading to this book are chronicled herein.

---

[1] *Colonial Mobile* by Peter J. Hamilton, page 310.

This book is self-edited by the author so the inevitable editing errors you will find are all mine. David Alsobrook director of the History Museum of Mobile considered my Fort Powell book to be "eclectic". No doubt he will consider this to be such also. Every researcher who feels compelled to reduce his files to what he hopes is a coherent book goes about such differently. I obviously do. Notwithstanding, I hope you'll find this book interesting and informative.

Captain William Pickles Society
Covington, Louisiana

Covington, louisiana

Battle on Lake Pontchartrain....

To prevent the British from reinforcing Baton Rouge it was necessary for the Spanish to secure control of the lakes. Britain maintained one armed sloop in Lake Pontchartrain appropriately named the "West Florida." In September 1779 a patched together ship of war commanded by Captain William Pickles engaged the West Florida and in a sharp and violent firefight captured her - ensuring that Glavez' expedition need fear no British reinforcements from Pensacola......see more about this and Bernardo de Galvez, the Louisiana hero of the American Revolution!

Captain William Pickles is recognized as the hero of the Battle of Lake Pontchartrain by at least one group on the north shore of the Lake- from the group's web site.

British West Florida

Mobile was a part of French Louisiana since its founding in 1702 with the Perdido River being the boundary line between French Louisiana and Spanish Florida. The Seven Years War (1754-63), known in North America as the French and Indian War, gave the British control of the area after Britain soundly defeated her traditional enemies France and Spain. Following that war the British held Havana and Manila which Spain desperately wanted to recover. In 1763 France ceded Louisiana (including Mobile) to Spain who then traded Florida together with the area from the Perdido River to the Mississippi River

North of Lake Pontchartrain and the Manchac or Bienville Rivers, to Britain in return for Havana, Manila and some scattered islands. The British then divided their new territory into East Florida and West Florida with their province of West Florida extending from the Chattahoochee to the Mississippi River with an initial northern boundary just south of Birmingham. The population of East Florida was concentrated along the east coast while that of West Florida was more scattered but with most of the population in Pensacola and Mobile.

The British made Pensacola the capital of West Florida because they considered it healthier and thought to be easier to defend than Mobile. Its harbor was the finest on the Gulf coast while oceangoing vessels could not come within several miles of Mobile.

In 1763 the British 22nd infantry Regiment occupied French Fort Condé built in 1717 at Mobile which they renamed Fort Charlotte. The brick Fort was in need of repair but was still the finest such structure on the northern Gulf coast while Pensacola was fortified only by a decaying wood palisade stockade. Mobile was, at the time home to about 40 French families of some 200 individuals. Ultimately 112 French Mobilians remained in British Mobile. During the period of British control, and particularly after the outbreak of the Revolutionary War loyalists and refugees settled in the Tensaw and Fort Toulouse area and on the Mississippi River at Manchac, Point Coupé, Baton Rouge and Natchez. The British appointed governors and a council which rarely met. They maintained regular garrisons at Mobile and Pensacola as well as small forces at Manchac[2] and later Baton Rouge and Natchez on the Mississippi River.

Pensacola had a fine harbor but the town depended entirely upon Mobile and its environs for its food crops and cattle. When Lieutenant Colonel Augustine Provost, commanding officer of the 60th regiment took possession of Pensacola from the Spanish on August 6, 1763 Provost expressed disappointment in the town. He said the country side was still uncultivated; the fort was a rotten stockade without a ditch and the barracks; "nothing more than miserable bark huts, without any sort of fireplaces or windows." But, Pensacola and Mobile had a substantial trade with the Indians and the British considered that the colony had a potential for profits, something the Spanish had never been able to produce from East Florida.[3]

George Johnstone first governor of British West Florida

---

[2] Manchac was defended by Frontier log-stockade built in 1765 and named Fort Bute in honor of the British Prime Minister. In July 1779, the British recognized it as indefensible and most of its garrison was withdrawn to Baton Rouge, *Honor and fidelity* by Jack D. L. Holmes, 1965.

North America after the Treaty of Paris 1763

---

[3] Robert V. Haynes, *The Natchez District and the American Revolution*, University Press of Mississippi, 1976.

The Colonies Revolt

In 1775 thirteen of the British colonies in North America revolted. The recently acquired Florida provinces along with Canada remained loyal to the Crown.

The Revolutionary War did not begin with dramatic suddenness; there were several years of political unrest and rioting. During that time many decided that war was a possibility, if not a certainty, long before actual hostilities began.[4] A number of those who anticipated the coming conflict moved to the West Florida frontier before the war. After the war began more Loyalists or Tories[5] then seeking to escape from the revolting Colonies fled to the West Florida frontier. The 1776 population of Mobile was estimated to be 860 persons most of which were the military garrison and their dependents. During the first three years of the war the British 16th infantry Regiment provided the garrison troops for the several West Florida forts.

---

[4] During the summer of 1774 even Samuel Adams of Boston was not convinced that war was imminent. A permanent rupture was not anticipated. *Bunker Hill, a City, a Siege, a Revolution* by Nathaniel Philbrick, page 120.

[5] They called themselves "Whigs".

During those first few years of the American Revolution, West Florida remained uninvolved and unmolested. Overtures were made to the population by the Continental Congress but such was rejected and loyalty professed to King George III. As a practical matter towns were garrisoned by redcoats and the few scattered homesteaders on the Tensaw, the Mississippi coast and around Natchez were far removed from the revolting Colonies, separated from them and under constant risk of attack by hostile Indians whose allegiance, if any, was to the British.

The rebelling Americans wanted to attack the British in West Florida. Early in the war at the urging of Oliver Pollock,[6] representative of Congress at New Orleans, the Continental Navy, then run by a committee of Congress, ordered an attack on Pensacola and the blockade of British interests in the Mississippi River. On February 1, 1777 John Paul Jones was given command of the ships *Alfred, Comet, Cabot, Hampden* and the sloop *Providence* for a cruise first to capture the Isle of St. Kitts in the West Indies and then to Pensacola to deal with two or three British sloops that were making a nuisance of themselves there and to seize the supply of cannon in the town then move to the mouth of the Mississippi River to capture any enemy vessels there. The fleet was then to proceed to Barbados or West Africa to capture British slavers. A tall order indeed.

---

[6] In May 1777 Spanish Governor Galvez offered to supply U.S. troops with cash and supplies if Congress would send an expedition against Pensacola and the Mississippi River. *Papers of the Continental Congress compiled 1774 – 1789,* U.S. Archives Washington D.C., record group 360.

Unfortunately, the British naval blockade prevented any of Jones' ships from getting to sea.[7] Until 1779 only privateers operating out of the East Coast and New Orleans made forays into the Gulf.[8]

If Congress could not attack British West Florida through its Gulf of Mexico front door then the Ohio/Mississippi River back door would have to suffice. The war was brought to West Florida by way of the Mississippi River in mid February 1778 when Marine Captain James Willing with his keelboat *Rattletrap* and his band of raiders reached the Natchez settlements.

The Willing raid coincided with the entry into the war by France and with the signing on February 6, 1778 of an alliance between the revolting United States and France. For the rest of the war the presence of French fleets in the Caribbean limited the availability of British naval reinforcements for West Florida.

---

[7] *The Life and Letters of John Paul Jones*, Vol. 1, page 142 by Mrs. Regin De Koven; *John Paul Jones: A Sailors Biography*, page 143, by Samuel Eliot Morison.

[8] *Records and Papers of Continental Congress*, 50, page 66; *The Navy of the American Revolution,* a dissertation by Charles Oscar Paullin, 1906.

The Willing Raid

James Willing was a member of a prominent Philadelphia family and brother to a member of the first Continental Congress. He had moved to a plantation just North of Baton Rouge in 1774. He was not successful as a merchant/planter and with mounting debts he returned to Pennsylvania in 1777. On the Mississippi River he was an agitator for the revolution which made him unpopular with many of his loyalist neighbors. Through the influence of his brother Thomas and close friend Robert Morris[9] he received a commission as Captain of Marines from Congress with authorization to organize a volunteer company of Marines at Fort Pitt. He was there to secure and arm a large boat; proceed down the Ohio and Mississippi Rivers where he was to take dispatches and to attempt to win the assistance or force the neutrality of all the inhabitants along the east bank of the Mississippi River (the British side) and then return to Fort Pitt,

---

[9] Robert Morris was known as "the financier of the American Revolution." He was a signer of the Declaration of Independence, the Articles of Confederation and the Constitution. He was a powerful committee chairman in the Continental Congress, an important figure in Pennsylvania politics, and perhaps the most prominent businessman of his day. Yet today he is probably the least known of the great national leaders of the revolutionary era.

conveying five boat loads of dry goods and arms that Spain had agreed to deliver at New Orleans for the cause.[10]

James Willing and the Rattletrap - 1778

Even though Wiling's exploits were included in the pictorial history *The Marines in the Revolution* and he described himself as having a commission in the Navy it is not clear from period records exactly to which branch of service he belonged. In various Congressional documents he was referred to as: "soldier", "naval captain" and a "marine". At Fort Pitt twenty-five experienced soldiers from the 13th Regiment of foot of the Virginia Continental Line volunteered to join Captain Wiling's expedition. The troops were told that they were "to go on some business to New Orleans". The armed boat *Rattletrap* was

---

[10] *The Marines in the Revolution, a Pictorial History*, History and Museums Division Headquarters, US Marine Corps, Washington DC, 1975; *Hupp Family Tales, Voyage of the Rattletrap, 1778* by Olin L Hupp, Internet publication.

assigned to Willing for that purpose.[11] Willing and his 34 man company departed Fort Pitt on the night of January 10, 1778.[12]

Willing made his way down the Ohio and Mississippi Rivers picking up volunteers as he went, avoiding the British in Illinois and successfully made his way to Natchez in February 1778. The Choctaw friends of the British had been tasked with watching the River along with a small British guard which was expected to have given a warning in advance of an incursion such as the Willing raid. The Choctaws had abandoned their posts and Willing easily captured the small British guard. The British had harsh words for their allies failure to warn the river towns of the approaching colonials and thereafter the Choctaw watch on the River was heightened. At Natchez Willing secured an agreement from the inhabitants that they would not take up arms against the United States.

An advance party under Captain McIntosh captured on the Mississippi River at Manchac the letter of Marque *Rebecca* which was armed with sixteen 4-pounder guns and several swivels. Instead of proceeding to New Orleans as originally planned Willing waited at Manchac for the arrival of his main force which was supplemented by several people from the Natchez settlement, a number of French and Spanish bateau men and some hunters and banditti. With those reinforcements the number of men in Willing's party then totaled nearly 200.

---

[11] The keelboat *Rattletrap* was similar to the keelboat used by Lewis and Clark on their expedition of exploration in 1805.
[12] *The Marines of the Revolution.*

South of Natchez the nature of the raid changed from securing the neutrality of the residents to burning, plundering and harassing the loyalist. As Willing approached his former homestead just north of Baton Rouge he began to treat his former neighbors harshly. Numerous plantations were looted or burned. Slaves and livestock were taken away but on a selective basis. Those considered as patriots were unmolested while those with British sympathies were pillaged. No one was killed but there were some close calls. Spanish territory was out of bounds for the raiders and was just across or down the river allowing the loyal planters to flee. The devastation wrought by Willing's men was almost complete at Baton Rouge with the British side of the river almost cleared of inhabitants.

The depredations committed by Willing's raiders against British settlers along the Mississippi River in West Florida instantly became a matter of controversy and has remained so ever since. The British considered the American raiders to be nothing but a group of outlaws and if they had been captured at the time it is not at all clear that they would have been treated as prisoners of war although Willing was later captured and was treated as such. Probably the uniformed Fort Pitt volunteers would have been treated likewise. Very few members of the expedition wore military uniforms; the vast majority were dressed in the style of hunters, armed with a rifle, cutlass and one or two pistols. Willing insisted he was a captain in the United States Navy and he treated his men if they were soldiers of the United States.

While the original group that enlisted at Fort Pitt were unquestionably military personnel the recruits he picked up down the river ranged from dedicated patriots to villains and freebooters. From Natchez south the confiscations and predations of the Willing party primarily hardened the resolve of the settlors to remain loyal to the Crown.

By March the raiding party arrived at New Orleans. But the pillaging was not confined to just one trip down the river. Groups consisting of several boatloads of the Willing party made several additional incursions into the territory between Manchac and Baton Rouge. These later expeditions, thought by the British in many instances to be contrary to previous neutrality agreements, so outraged the population that it was all but impossible for the residents to remain as impartial after the coming of James Willing as it had before his onslaught.

Meanwhile, Oliver Pollock was laying the groundwork for the expected arrival of Wiling's party in New Orleans. Since 1768, when he first came to Louisiana, Pollock had cultivated the friendship of the successive Spanish governments, and was on exceptionally good terms with Governor Galvez who had occupied that post since 1 January 1777. Pollock referred to Galvez as: "that worthy Noble-man" and stated that he "gave me the delightful assurance that he would go every possible link for the interest of Congress." [13]

---

[13] *The Navy of the American Revolution* by Charles Oscar Paullin, Cleveland, the Burrows Brothers Company, 1906.

As soon as he learned of Willing's approach, sometime in February 1777, Pollock called on the Governor and made arrangements for a friendly reception for Willing's party. He also dispatched his nephew, Thomas Pollock with a party of 15 volunteers from New Orleans to assist Willing in capturing the British ship *Rebecca*. Lieutenant McIntyre and his raiders had already accomplished that objective by the time young Pollock and his men reached Manchac, so they then cooperated with Willing's party in the plundering on the British side of the river.

Spain was not then at war with Britain and a strong protest was lodged with Governor Galvez by the British for harboring the marauders. British vessels captured in Spanish territory were returned to their owners. British vessels, such as the *Rebecca*, captured in British waters and brought to New Orleans and any territory seized and held by the Colonials posed a problem for Governor Galvez. Galvez wrote to his uncle, the Spanish Secretary of State, that his Lordship had forewarned him that if the Colonials seized the British settlements along the River and desired to deliver them to his Spanish Majesty they should be accepted in trust provided there would be no violent response from the British. He was instructed to advise the British that it was better that the settlements be under control of the King of Spain than to be in the hands of their Colonial enemies.[14]

Under the urging of Pollock, Governor Galvez issued an edict "offering protection to both sides should they flee to the city of New Orleans" and permitting the inhabitants of Louisiana

---

[14] *Naval Records of the Revolution*, volume 11, page 836.

to extend "hospitality and asylum to the refugees." Although this proclamation was ostensibly designed to maintain "the strict neutrality of Spain" towards both belligerents, no one was misled by Galvez's careful choice of language since his obvious purpose was to allow Willing and his men freedom of the city. Galvez responded to Willing's request to house some of his people in private homes in Spanish territory by offering him the use of a public building as barracks for his soldiers. His excuse was that humanity demanded it and besides; "the petitioning men held guns "and Galvez thought it best to appease them.

Equally controversial was Galvez's decision to permit the disposal of Willing's plunder in New Orleans at public auction. The Governor partially justified this flagrant violation of Spanish law to his superiors in Madrid on the grounds that desperately needed duties would be paid on the indigo and peltries which they had "salvaged" and that the inhabitants would be able to purchase experienced slaves at bargain prices as the most valuable portion of the confiscated property consisted of approximately 680 slaves.

The proceeds from the plunder amounted to some $62,500 plus another $37,500 assigned for the ship *Rebecca* which was bought for Congress by Oliver Pollock to be fitted out and commissioned under American colors. She was to join several smaller Spanish vessels in protecting New Orleans against any British attack and eventually to transport the Willing party to Philadelphia.

Although Willing's party was the principal raiding group on the lower Mississippi others joined in. A group of 26 boatmen, recruited in New Orleans by Captain Paul Lafitte, proceeded down the Mississippi River, picking up a large number of Americans on the way, where they attacked and captured the English brig *Neptune* anchored near the river's mouth. According to some of the *Neptune's* passengers the boatman: " were armed with cutlasses and they wore either cockades or deer tails in their hats."

Vincente Rillieux of New Orleans led a small sloop up the Amite River from Lake Pontchartrain as far as Bayou Manchac where he landed his small force and ambushed an English barque. Believing themselves attacked by superior numbers, the sailors fled below deck. Rillieux and his men boarded the vessel, sealed the hatches and triumphantly sailed to New Orleans with 12 sailors and 56 Germans from the Waldecker Regiment. Rillieux's own forces numbered 14.[15]

A privateer schooner, the *Reprisal,* was fitted out by Oliver Pollock and placed under the command of Joseph Calvert. On March 24 the *Reprisal* seized the British schooner *Dispatch* above Southwest Pass near the mouth of the Mississippi River with a cargo of 50 slaves and 100 barrels of flour, two barrels of sugar and one barrel of coffee. After disposing of most of the slaves at one plantation Calvert brought the rest to Oliver Pollock's estate near Baton Rouge were some were sold and the remaining divided among the captors.[16] This is not the last we hear of Joseph Calvert. In February 1781 when Galvez and the

---

[15] *Honor and fidelity* by Jack D.L. Holmes, 1965, page 31.
[16] Robert V. Haynes, *The Natchez District and the American Revolution.*

Spanish fleet sailed from Havana to besiege Pensacola it was accompanied by the American privateer sloop *Terrible* under the command of Captain Calvert.[17]

As a consequence of the Willing raid the British reinforcements to West Florida enabled the British and their Indian allies to establish a near blockade of the Mississippi River which prevented the sending of supplies upstream to the Revolution and the English side of the Mississippi was lost back to the King. Willing was to have engaged five or six boats to ship government cargo back up river but the British blockade prevented that and Pollock had to arrange for transportation by sea.[18]

Because of the increased British presence on the River, Galvez insisted that Willing's men not return to the Ohio through West Florida so as to avoid more contact and conflict with the British. Willing's Virginia Continental line troopers proceeded back north through Arkansas to St. Louis where they were placed under the command of Gen. George Rogers Clark. The troops walked most of the way. The *Morris* (ex *Rebecca*) outfitted as a cruiser was to have been available to carry Willing and his raiders back home but unfortunately she was lost in the 1779 hurricane.[19]

---

[17] *Wars of the Americas: A Chronology of Armed Conflict in the New World,* 1492, by David F. Marley, 1998.

[18] The boats were to have been shallow draft, well manned and armed with swivels or cohorns (mortars) and muskets.

[19] *Bernardo de Galvez in Louisiana 1776 – 1783* by J. W. Caughey.

Willing is reported to have made his way to the Tensaw territory north of Mobile where it is alleged, by Mobile historian Peter Joseph Hamilton in his book *Colonial Mobile*[20] that he distributed copies of the *Declaration of Independence* but secured no uprising against the crown. He embarked on a sloop bound for Philadelphia. The sloop was captured off the Capes of Delaware and Willing was taken prisoner and imprisoned in New York.[21] Toward the end of 1779 he was exchanged for British Colonel Henry Hamilton.[22] It is not at all clear that Willing actually reached the Tensaw territory.

The American raids, and what appeared to the British to be Spanish complicity, naturally infuriated the British in West Florida. In an effort to put forth at least the appearance of neutrality Galvez on March 3, 1778 issued an order that he was observing strict neutrality as to the party of "America

---

[20] Page 311, Hamilton states: "It is said that Pollock came with Willing to Mobile, and brought the *Declaration of Independence* for distribution. This famous document was then contraband of war, and Willing soon found himself a prisoner in Fort Charlotte. He remained in irons there until exchanged in 1779 for Col. Hamilton, at Detroit."

[21] *Papers of the Continental Congress* compiled 1774 – 1789, record group 360.

[22] *Voyage of the Rattletrap, 1778*, an internet publication by Olin L. Hupp; *Our Countries' First Marines and my Fourth Great-Grandfather Jacob Wheat, Gunner age 17, January 1778* an internet publication by Olin L. Hupp; *Willing's Expedition Down the Mississippi, 1778* by John Caughey, Louisiana historical Quarterly, January 1932.

Englishmen proceeding south on the Mississippi River" (referring to Willing's party).[23]

The incursion of James Willing down the Mississippi had mixed results. Some British vessels were removed from the River but troop reinforcements to Baton Rouge and Natchez closed the Mississippi to supplies for the Revolution. In the autumn of 1778 about 1200 British regulars, Waldeckers (Germans) and Provincials, under Maj. Gen. John Campbell had been sent to reinforce the garrisons of West Florida. On a positive note those British reinforcements sent to West Florida in response to the Willing raid tied up troops that could have been profitably used against General Washington's forces in the main theaters of war.

Major General John Campbell

---

[23] *Naval Records of the Revolution,* volume 11, page 503.

Oliver Pollock

Oliver Pollock – The New Orleans Connection

The Continental Congress, then acting through committees, was fortunate to have Oliver Pollock[24] as its commercial agent in New Orleans. Pollock's devotion to the revolution and his friendship with the Spanish Governors at New Orleans served them well.

Oliver Pollock was born in Ireland about 1737 and immigrated to Carlisle, Pennsylvania about 1760. Some two years later he moved to Havana, Cuba where he was connected with a prominent mercantile house. He was a Roman Catholic. Through the influences of Father Butler, the president of the Jesuit College in Havana he became a close friend of Don Alexander O'Reilly, the Governor General of Cuba. In 1762 France ceded Louisiana to Spain. By 1768 Pollock, probably at the suggestion of O'Reilly, had moved to New Orleans which

---

[24] There are numerous books, papers and websites relating to Oliver Pollock. *The Historical Register: Notes and Queries, Historical and Genealogical, Relating to Interior Pennsylvania, for the year 1883*, volume 1, printed in 1883, states that Pollock's private papers, including all of his official documents and correspondence with the Continental Congress were destroyed during the Civil War – partly at Vicksburg, Mississippi and partly by the U. S. Gunboat *Essex*, when it shelled Bayou Sara, Louisiana in 1863. His letters to Congress are contained in The *Papers of the Continental Congress compiled 1774 – 1789*, record group 360.

had then a population of about 8000 and offered to the well-connected and energetic Pollock an excellent prospect for his mercantile business. In New Orleans he soon established his reputation. He made frequent voyages to the east coast and established a trade with Spain and France.

In 1769 he fitted out in Baltimore a brig, which he named the *Royal Charlotte*, and loaded her with flour for New Orleans. Meanwhile his friend O'Reilly had been appointed Captain General and Governor of the Province of Louisiana. The French population of Louisiana was understandably not happy that their King had transferred Louisiana to the King of Spain. They revolted and on August 17, 1769 Pollock's friend O'Reilly, then considered one of the best generals in Spanish service, arrived at New Orleans with 8000 troops thereby doubling the population of the town and causing an immediate shortage of food. The provisions O'Reilly had ordered to be forwarded had not arrived, and a famine was imminent. At that propitious moment Pollock sailed into port with his load of flour. Before his arrival the last barrels had sold for $30. Pollock immediately placed his entire cargo at the disposal of the Governor and requested O'Reilly to fix the price. The governor refused to do so. As Pollock did not wish to take advantage of the situation he offered the flour at $15 per barrel which was readily agreed to. O'Reilly made a note to the King of Pollock's generosity and gave him free trading rights within all of the Spanish Louisiana. This concession was the foundation of Pollock's large fortune, which he subsequently placed at the disposal of the Colonies.

When open warfare between the Colonists and the mother country erupted in 1775 Pollock was the most prominent and energetic English merchant residing in New Orleans. His sympathies were with the Revolution to which he immediately offered his services. In 1777 he was appointed as commercial agent of the United States Government in New Orleans, essentially making him the representative of the Congress. In 1778 and 1779 he borrowed $70,000 from Spanish Louisiana's then governor Bernardo de Galvez with which he purchased supplies including 10,000 pounds of powder and uniforms in support of American military operations west of the Mississippi, including George Rogers Clark's campaign in Illinois in 1778. In addition to money from Spain much of his enormous private wealth was used or loaned to assist the Revolution. Some of the stores purchased from Spain were to have been sent up river to Fort Pitt by Captain Willing.

On July 10, 1776, Don Bernardo de Galvez, then Colonel of the Regiment of Louisiana, was appointed provisional governor. He was a young man of talent, energy and character, the son of the then Viceroy of Mexico and the nephew of the Spanish Secretary of State. Pollock and Galvez became good friends, the former naming his son Galvez in honor of the governor. Pollock later served Galvez as an Aid-De-Camp in his campaigns against the British in West Florida.[25] Galvez requested that Pollock accompany him on his expedition to

---

[25] *The Pollock Family of Pennsylvania*, Historical Register; *Notes and Queries Historical and Genealogical, Relating to Interior Pennsylvania for the year 1883*, volume 1; *Clan Pollock International: Oliver Pollock, Unsung Hero of the American revolution*, Internet site.

Manchac and Baton Rouge and offered him a commission as a Colonel In the service of Spain. Pollock declined and took to the field under his Continental flag along with nine "brother Americans."[26]

Pollock, as commercial agent of Congress at New Orleans, also had supervision of naval affairs on the Mississippi River and was authorized to commission both vessels and officers for Continental service as well as commissioning privateers. Pollock had commissioned at least one privateer for in 1777 Pollock captured a British vessel containing 200 slaves. In 1778 the *Joseph*, a vessel outfitted by James willing and Oliver Pollock, captured the British schooner *Dispatch*, a slaver from Jamaica.[27]

---

[26] *Papers of the Continental Congress compiled 1774 – 1789* , letters from Oliver Pollock, record group 360.

[27] *The Economy of British West Florida 1763-1783* by Robin A. Fabel, University of Alabama Press, 1988.

The Morris

The ship *Rebecca*, had been taken in early March 1778 on the Mississippi River at Manchac by ten continentals from Willing's party under the command of Lieutenant Thomas McIntyre of the Independent Company of Western Pennsylvania. The *Rebecca* was a British letter of Marque that had been fitted out in London. The Rebecca mounted 16 carriage guns (four pounders) and six swivels with a crew of 20 men on board. The prize was brought by Captain Willing to New Orleans in April 1778.[28] Pollock purchased the vessel for Congress at her appraised value of $4780. His initial plan was that the vessel, after being fully converted as a warship, could convoy vessels from New Orleans to the east coast as she would be able to cope with any of the British warships then stationed at Pensacola.[29] The ship was also to return Willing and his raiders to the east coast.

---

[28] *Naval Documents of the American Revolution*, volume 11, pages 492 – 93, minutes of the Governor's Council of West Florida, March 2, 1778. The Rebecca was built in Newfoundland in 1773, owned by G.E. Montgomery of London and under the command of Captain John Cox. *Papers of the Continental Congress compiled 1774 – 1789*, record group 360.

[29] *Papers of the Continental Congress Compiled 1774 – 1789*, record group 360.

As the *Rebecca* had been originally designed as an armed cruiser Captain Pickles thought she would make a fine ship of war by taking out her upper deck. Pollock began collecting a crew and employed Captain Pickles in fitting out the *Rebecca* as a ship of war for the American Navy at a cost of $23,500. Refitted as a warship she was commissioned into the Navy as the *Morris,* named after Pollock's friend and business associate Robert Morris of Philadelphia.[30]

Pollock attempted to purchase 24 pounders to arm the *Morris* from Havana, but the Spanish authorities refuse to permit the shipment even after Galvez had written to the Cuban government requesting such.[31] Notwithstanding, by July, 1779 Pollock had succeeded in obtaining and mounting twenty-four guns on the decks of the ship which he had by then christened the "*Morris*". The ships 4-pounders were replaced with a battery of sixteen 6-pounders on one deck, 2 bow and 2 stern chasers and eight 4-pounders on her quarterdeck together with swivels. Captain William Pickles was placed in command of the *Morris* with Pierre George Rousseau named as first officer.[32]

---

[30] Morris, of Philadelphia, was a politician and signer of the Declaration of Independence.
[31] *The Navy of the American Revolution* by Charles Oscar Paullin, page 309.
[32] *The American Sailing Navy,* by Howard I. Chapell, page 96.

Captain William Pickles

Captain William Pickles[33] was commissioned a captain in the Continental Navy on October 10, 1776. At the time Congress was trying to purchase blankets and other articles for the army in New Orleans. Pickles first naval service involved the conveyance of funds for that purpose from Philadelphia to New Orleans. There he first met Oliver Pollock.

Willing, Morris and Company of Philadelphia agreed to supply Congress with $30,000 provided they would repay the same in Europe. Accordingly two drafts of $15,000 each were entrusted to Captain Pickles to deliver to New Orleans. Duplicates were sent by Captain James Le Mair who disappeared never arriving in New Orleans. Pickles embarked as supercargo from Charleston on the schooner *Lewis*, under the command of Captain Rowan, but the crew of the vessel mutinied and took it into New Providence, Bahamas after placing Captain Rowan and Pickles ashore on the coast at

---

[33] The first historical reference found of Captain William Pickles was a notation in the *South- Carolina and American General Gazette* dated December 16, 1774 noting that on the previous day Captain Pickles along with others sailed for London in the ship *Carolina* – Packet.

Matanzas in Cuba. The bills never reached New Orleans."[34] Pickles eventually made his way to New Orleans.

In 1777 Pickles was master of the brig *Norton*. In April 1777 the Spanish authorities at New Orleans captured the *Norton* but later returned it to Pickles.

Pollock used him as a courier as exhibited by an October 24, 1777 letter written by the Commerce Committee of the Continental Congress to Pollock acknowledging receipt of his letters by Captain Pickles.[35] The Committee sent to Pollock blank commissions for privateers with bonds and instructions for his use as their agent. The committee wanted goods purchased for Congress by Pollock sent by sea as it took too long, was too expensive, too heavy and subject to being taken by Indians if sent up River to Fort Pitt. "Captain Pickles tells us he has a fine brigantine suitable for bringing a cargo along the coast – if that be so and the Governor and you should thank him a proper person we will agree." Pollock agreed with the Committee as to Pickles reliability.[36]

---

[34] *Naval Documents of the American Revolution*, U.S. Navy Historical Section, US Government Printing Office, volume 7, page 98 (note); *Naval Documents of the American Revolution*, volume 11, page 519; *The South Carolina and American General Gazette*, Thursday, March 5, 1778.

[35] *Naval Documents of the American Revolution*, Volume 10, pages 266 – 67.

[36] *The Navy of the American Revolution*, volume 10, pages 560 – 61.

Spain Declares War against Britain

Bernardo de Galvez

On June 21, 1779 Spain formally declared war against Britain and renewed her old alliance with France in warring against their common historical enemy.[37] On July 8, 1779, the American subjects of Spanish King Charles III in the New World learned they were to take part in the war.

---

[37] Some Louisiana historians give the date of the war declaration as May 8, 1779; *Standard history of New Orleans Louisiana* edited by Henry Richtor, Chicago 1900; *The History of Louisiana* by Francois-Xavier Martin, New Orleans, 1882.

The King of Spain should have had no interest in supporting revolution in the Americas. A popular revolution to overthrow the authority of a king, any king, in America was the King of Spain's worst nightmare. Even the adage: "my enemies enemy is my friend" was of doubtful application. What Spain was interested in was discomforting England. Spain never entered into any formal alliance[38] with the rebelling colonists although France did.

Spain declared war on England not to assist the American Revolution but allied with France they saw the opportunity to recover Cuba, Manila and other scattered former colonies. Ever since the Seven Years War France and Spain were building up their navies while England's decayed. The timing seemed right to renew hostilities with their traditional enemy.

Popular uprisings overthrowing kings anywhere in the western world was also not in the interest of the King of France. The model for representative government in the U. S. subsequently spread to France where the King lost his throne and his head. The interest of the King of France in the American Revolution was also simply to discomfort England and the French alliance with the revolutionaries was to distract the British and draw away military assets to assist in the avenging of the defeat suffered in the Seven Years War (1757 – 1763). Both France and Spain focused on the short-term benefits of North American revolution as a distraction to England and lost sight of

---

[38] Although there was no formal alliance there was certainly a de-facto one.

the threat that the example of a free and democratic United States posed to totalitarian regimes.

Nevertheless, and regardless of the soundness of their intentions, the aid supplied by Spain to the revolting colonies was substantial and that supplied by France was crucial to the success of the revolution.

Since prior to the time of the Willing raid both the British governor in Pensacola and Governor Galvez in New Orleans were anticipating the looming war and were preparing to invade each other's territory.

Upon opening of hostilities Galvez wanted to immediately attack British West Florida but as was the custom brought the question before a council of war. The proposition was rejected and the Council recommended that until reinforcements could be obtained from Havana only defensive measures should be adopted. Ignoring his counsel Galvez readied his regular troops, the militia volunteered their services and an army of about 1430 men, including 160 Indians, was collected.[39] Galvez also had a small fleet under his direct command, composed of one schooner and three gunboats. With these forces Galvez decided to move up the Mississippi River immediately.[40] Galvez may have been ready but the weather did not cooperate.

---

[39] *History of Louisiana* by Francois-Xavier Martin, page 227.
[40] *Standard History of New Orleans* edited by Henry Rightor, 1900.

Map of lower Mississippi River

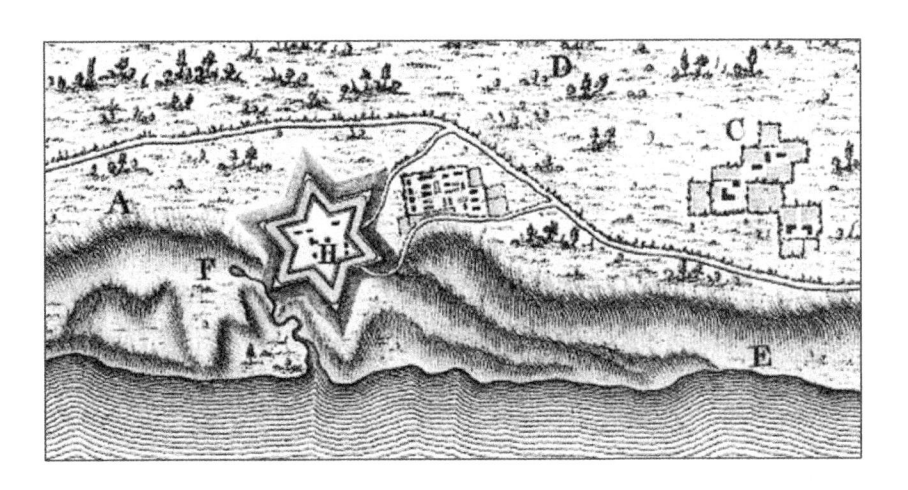

Plan of Fort at Baton Rouge

A hurricane struck the New Orleans area on August 18, 1779 damaging and sinking a number of ships in the Mississippi River including the colonial vessel *Rebecca*, renamed the *Morris* by Pollock. The vessel had been fully outfitted and armed with 24 guns. She was fully manned and ready for sea with a crew of

56 under the command of Captain Pickles. Eleven of her crew were lost. Fortunately Captain Pickles survived.[41]

It is apparent that the Spanish, or at least Governor Galvez, was ready for immediate action upon the commencement of war. Major general John Campbell the British commander of West Florida, headquartered at Pensacola, also had plans to launch an immediate attack on the Spanish at New Orleans upon the anticipated declaration of war. However, the British underestimated the will and resourcefulness of their adversary.

The Spanish preemptive strike against the British settlements on the Mississippi River was underway before the British commander learned that hostilities had commenced. The success of Galvez's forces and the distress of the British is best shown by the following report from Maj. General John Campbell at Pensacola to his commander General Sir Henry Clinton in New York dated September 14, 1779. This report follows a previous one in which he pointed out his inability to execute Lord George Germains orders to immediately attack New Orleans upon opening of hostilities.

"I am sorry to have to inform your Excellency, that the fears expressed in my letter of the 11th instance have proved true – a dispatch I this moment have received from Lieutenant Colonel Dickson informs me, that on the 20th ultimo the Independence of the American States was publickly declared by

---

[41] *The History of the American Sailing Navy* by Howard I. Chapelle, page 96.

beat of drum at New Orleans; That on the 29th of the same month, two of our transports that were returning from the Amite River, where they had landed a detachment of the regiment of Waldeck were seized at Galvez Town, and it would appear that they intended to have kept this last transaction a secret from Colonel Dixon, and Governor Galvez was marching with a considerable force towards Manchac, on the pretense that our collecting troops at that place, rendered such a measure on his part absolutely necessary; but at the same time professing the greatest cordiality and friendship, and expressing his hopes that satisfactory reasons would be given him for our movement; his intentions would appear to have been an endeavor to lull Colonel Dixon into a state of confidence and security whatever might be his intentions they were fortunately frustrated by a deserter from the enemy (an Hibernian[42]) who gave information as above, and with Col. Dixon on his guard: however I am sorry to add that I find he has considered himself under the necessity of destroying a vessel load of provisions, that had been lately sent for the troops under his command, and which he had not had time to convey to Manchac, in order to prevent its falling into the enemy's hands; and as his store at Manchac was nearly expended he is left almost destitute of salt provisions and must depend on what he can procure from the inhabitants: Colonel Dixon further informs me that redoubt and some lines that have been lately thrown up at Messers Watt's and Flower's plantation on Baton Rouge intended for a post for the Regiment of Waldeck - being much more tenable and secure than the insignificant Fort at Manchac, he intended to desert

---

[42] An Irishman

and destroy the latter, after removing his stores and small remnant of provisions and to take post at the former place, which undoubtedly is strong by nature and has a better command of the Mississippi.

"Other misfortunes have happened on this occasion, a vessel laden with 300 barrels of provisions and a considerable quantity of rum, on her way to Manchac by the River Mississippi, has unquestionably fallen into the enemy's hands; and I dare not hope a better fate to two transports forwarded by the Lakes, – One with 55 officers and men of the Regiment of Waldeck, the other with provisions: in short the troops under Colonel Dickson's immediate command and at the Natchez consisting (besides officers) of 16 sergeants – 12 drummers and 429 rank-and-file are disagreeably and critically situated; the communication whereby to supply them with provisions entirely cut off, and the choice of methods of relieving them left for me to take one and all of them dangerous and uncertain in the execution: besides even Indians, for want of presents to make them, and for want of provisions on the Mississippi, cannot I'm afraid be employed for their relief; moreover the Indian Department is in confusion for want of Mr. Cameron the new Superintendent's arrival from the Cherokee nation (for which he was deputy) and after the alterations it has lately undergone, it is not yet recovered its wonted vigor.

"Since the date of my letter of the 11th I have had an account taken of the number of troops the vessels in this harbor fit for transports in the Lakes can carry, and the report made to me is 200 men with ease – and perhaps 50 more by crowding them; I have sent to Mobile to take for us what vessels can be found there, for this service and shall at all events proceed with as many troops as transports can be found for, to ship. I stand and act from thence as circumstances may direct or necessity required; but I have to prepare your Excellency for an event that will (if our conjectures proved true) frustrate and disappoint every plan we can project, either for the annoyance of the Enemy, or for carrying relief to Colonel Dickson; I have certain information that a large schooner was seen entering Lake Pontchartrain on the 9th instant – and, as there can be no idea formed of her, but being an Enemy's vessel, the *West Florida* armed sloop (our only force on the Lakes) carrying only four 3 & 4 pounders must fall a prey to her superior force, besides the Spaniards can now arm the four vessels they have taken as before represented and which are at Galvez Town, which will render them stronger on the lakes that any force we can fit out against them.[43]

"I have to report to your Excellency a step I've taken which perhaps may meet with censure, and may occasion some inconvenience, but as it proceeded from a persuasion and desire of thereby promoting the good of his Majesty's service; I hope (even if disapproved) that it will meet with the most favorable construction; – the *Carteret* packet boat being a ship of force carrying 18 six pounder's and 60 men, And there being

---

[43] The obvious conclusion to be drawn from this letter is that if the *West Florida* was lost on the Lake the Province of West Florida would be cut in half and General Campbell could not then reinforce, resupply or communicate by water with his forces on the Mississippi River.

no ship of war serviceable on the station, I made application to Governor Peter Chester in Counsel for an order to detain her, and which his counsel having unanimously approved, he has complied with, And I expect she will sail in a few days for the Balize[44] to discover whether any of the enemy ships are on that station or on this coast, and to endeavor finding out whether reinforcements have been sent them from the Havannah. This intelligence will be absolutely necessary to regulate my future conduct.

"Your Excellency will, from the full representation of the military state of this Province contained in this and in my letter of the 11th instance and from the knowledge of the other important objects of your command, be the best judge of whether a reinforcement to me is proper or expedient."[45]

General Campbell did not get his reinforcements, land or sea. The British garrison of West Florida was on its own. The Mississippi River forts and towns were lost in the first few months of war. The British had been surprised and placed on the defensive by the young and brash Governor Bernardo Galvez.

On August 27, 1779 Galvez moved on Manchac with 667 men. On the way up River he enlisted an additional 600 men and 160 Indians bringing his total force to 1427. In the eleven day march from New Orleans at least a third of that number was lost to fatigue and disease.

---

[44] Mouth of the Mississippi River.

[45] *Report on American Manuscripts in the Royal Institution of Great Britain*, Volume 2, 1906, page 31 – 33.

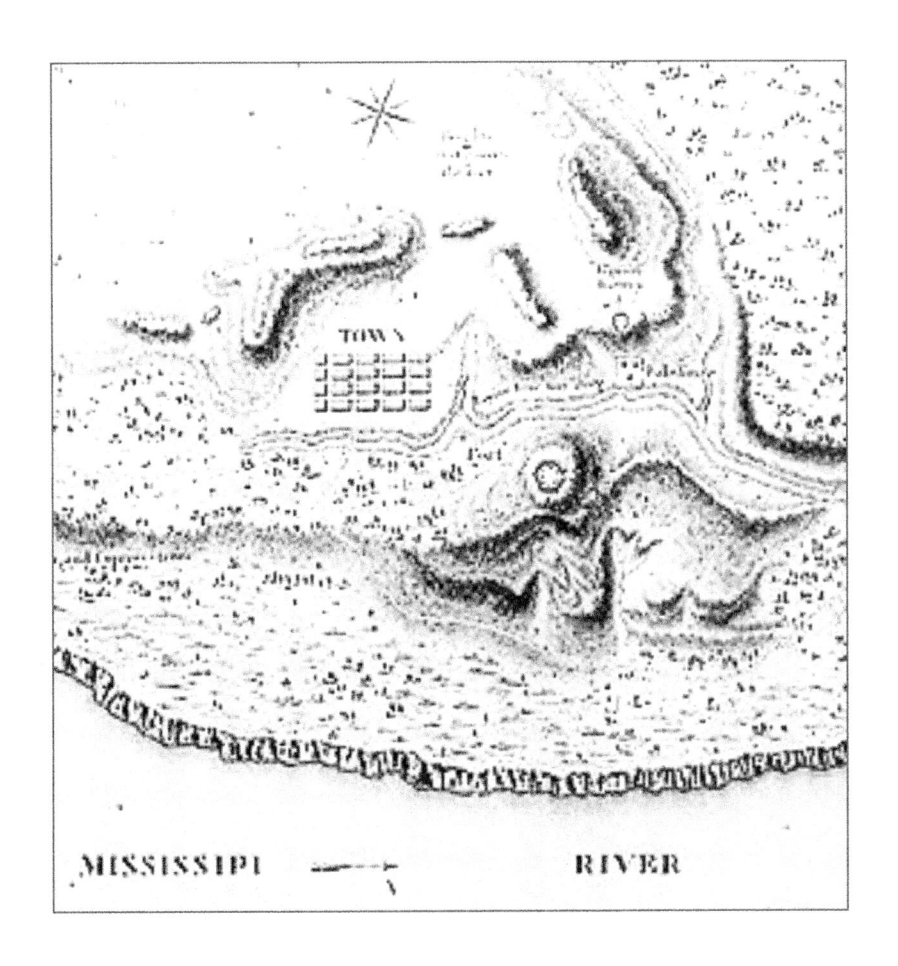

Town and Fort of Natchez

In the spring of 1765 the British had built Fort Bute on the Mississippi River on the north side of Bayou Manchac. It was abandoned and then reoccupied in December 1766. In 1767 the

Spanish built a small stockade called Fort San Gabriel de Manchac about 100 yards away on the southern side of the Bayou.

Both forts were abandoned then reoccupied in 1776. A small English settlement called Manchac developed near Fort Bute.[46]

Fort Bute, with 20 prisoners, was captured at dawn on September 7 when the Spanish rushed the Fort and took it from it's shocked twenty-seven man English garrison without the loss of a single Spaniard. The British loss was one killed and sixteen captured.[47] The Spanish force remained at Fort Bute for seven days then moved then to Baton Rouge which was defended by 146 Redcoats, 201 Waldecker's, 11 Royal Artillerymen and 150 armed settlers and negroes in a stout fort with thirteen cannon.

The force under Galvez had by then been reduced to 384 regular infantry, 14 artillerymen and 400 militia, Indians and negroes. By ruse Galvez was able to place a battery within musket shot. After a three hour cannonade the British were forced to capitulate on September 20, 1779. Natchez was included in the capitulation with Baton Rouge. Captured were

---

[46] *The Lakes of Pontchartrain Their History and Environments* by Robert W. Hastings.

[47] *History of Louisiana: The Spanish domination, Volume 3,* by Charles Gayarre.

375 prisoners from Baton Rouge and 80 from Natchez. For his efforts Galvez was promoted to brigadier general.[48]

The Spanish had struck the first blow and captured the west half of British West Florida.

The Western Theatre

---

[48] *The Regiment of Louisiana and the Spanish Army in thRevolution* by Thomas E. DeVoe and Gregory J. W. Urwin.

The British Naval Situation in West Florida

The British naval units on the northern Gulf Coast operated out of Pensacola. The Pensacola station was under the command of the Admiral in charge of the Gulf and Caribbean with headquarters at Port Royal, Jamaica. When more than one vessel was present at Pensacola the senior captain became the commander of all vessels there. In 1776 only one sloop was maintained in Pensacola as the only vessel in West Florida.[49] With the Revolutionary war and then the war with France the few ships available at Jamaica for service in the northern Gulf were overextended in cruising, escorting convoys, guarding the harbors, carrying supplies and troops and maintaining a presence on Lakes Pontchartrain and Maurepas to protect the trade route between Mobile and Pensacola and the Mississippi River settlements.

The American raid down the Mississippi in the winter and spring of 1778 caused alarm throughout West Florida. Governor Chester appealed to the navy and military authorities

---

[49] *Naval Records of the Revolution*, Volume 5, page 521, report of Vice Admiral Clark Gayton, Jamaica, June 13, 1776. Vice Admiral Clark Gayton was replaced in July 1777 by Admiral Sir Peter Parker as commander of the Jamaica station. *Naval Records of the Revolution*, volume 9, page 329. When Admiral Rodney and the British fleet was in the Caribbean Admiral Parker was subordinate to him. *The Economy of British West Florida*, page 149.

in Jamaica for reinforcements. In response Admiral Sir Peter Parker sent to Pensacola the survey schooner *Florida*[50], converted to combat use with eight guns, and allowed the war sloops *Hound* and *Sylph*, temporarily stationed in West Florida to remain there and temporarily assigned the frigate *Active* of 28 Guns. Another war sloop, the *Stork*, was also promised. These vessels were small, and some were rotten. They were hardly adequate to defend the lengthy coastline and waterways of West Florida, but they were a great deal better than nothing.[51] Maintaining and manning a vessel in isolated West Florida was difficult. The British Navy wanted to impress sailors there but that practice was not allowed by the Governor.

In 1778 the British sloop *Stork* provided the protection for Mobile Bay. A group of Willing's raiders entered Mobile Bay in three bateaus[52] and took away the merchant brig *Chance* laden with a cargo of staves. Lieutenant Kirkland commanding the *Florida* wanted to retake the brig, reportedly held at Ship Island, but he only had six men fit for duty. He obtained some sailors from the *Active* and 20 soldiers from the Pensacola

---

[50] The survey schooner *Florida* is not the same vessel at the sloop *West Florida*.

[51] *The Economy of British West Florida, 1763 – 1783*, by Robin F. A. Fabel, University of Alabama Press, 1988, page 149.

[52] Usually these vessels were propelled principally by oars but at least two of the three sent to Mobile Bay were schooner rigged which means they were equipped with a couple of masts and sails. One of them cut out the merchant brig *Chance* from her anchorage in Mobile Bay. According to Fabel the British authorities were unable to recover the brig or her cargo. *The Economy of British West Florida, 1763 – 1783* by Robin F. A. Fabel, page 63.

garrison to fill out his crew but was unsuccessful in retaking the *Chance*.

West Florida was not a priority for the overextended British Navy in 1178. Pensacola was not equipped to maintain a large force. The small number of ships sent to defend Mobile and Pensacola had not a chance of doing so against the Spanish fleet operating out of Havana.

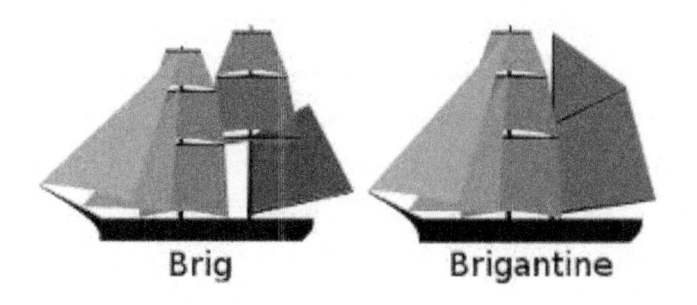

        Brig   Brigantine

HMS Sloop *West Florida*

To augment the naval force at Pensacola Admiral Gayton reported from Jamaica on June 13, 1776 that he had purchased a sloop of about 60 tons and drawing 6 feet of water abaft.[53] He named her the *West Florida*, placed Lieutenant George Burden in command and began fitting her out for service. By August 5, 1776 Gayton reported that the *West Florida* was ready to sail from Jamaica for what he considered to be an important station on the "Lakes of the Mississippi." By September 2 the "armed sloop" *West Florida* had arrived at Pensacola and was then the only vessel there. By September 19, 1776 The *Diligence*, a sloop of 14 guns, had arrived and the *West Florida* was released to proceed to her station on the Lakes.[54]

Smithsonian curator and maritime historian Howard I. Chapelle writes that many British Revolutionary War vessels classed as "sloops" were really schooners or cutters or brigs. During the Napoleonic wars vessel class nomenclature became fixed but not so in Revolutionary times. During the Napoleonic wars a "sloop of war" was a three-masted vessel with about 18 to 20 guns all on one deck. The *West Florida* was variously

---

[53] A 60 ton vessel of the period would be about 50 foot in length.

[54] *Naval Records of the Revolution*, Volume 9; Pollock referred to HMS *Diligence* a "sloop of war" in *Papers of the Continental Congress compiled 1774 – 1789*, record group 360.

described as a "sloop" or a "war sloop" which tells nothing about the arrangement of her masts, sails, decks or armament.[55] In July 1777 Admiral Gayton reported that HMS armed sloop *West Florida* and the *Florida*, which he called "surveying ships", were on their station on the Lakes: "agreeable to their lordships orders."[56] It is difficult today to imagine how hard such duty was. 20 to 40 men on a small vessel under 60 feet in length spending month after month, summer and winter, on Lake Pontchartrain. In the winter it would be cold and July, August and September incredibly hot notwithstanding the canvas awnings that would have undoubtedly been in place. Around her bulwarks would have been hung netting for repelling any attacker who might try to board. They would live off salt pork, hardtack bread and fish caught with their own seines. *The log of HMS Mentor 1780 – 1781*[57] is a good description of the daily operations of a larger sister vessel operating out of Pensacola.

The *West Florida* occasionally returned to Pensacola. On May 14, 1777 she arrived there from the Lakes after taking several prizes.[58] War between Spain and Britain was a year in the future but cold war like tensions were growing in the region. Reacting to the Spanish vessels taken by the *West Florida*

---

[55] Howard I. Chapelle, *The Baltimore Clipper*, page 32; See also Chapelle's *The History of the American Sailing Navy* and his companion work *The History of American Sailing Ships*.

[56] *Documents of the American Revolution*, volume 10, page 294.

[57] Edited by James A. Servies, published by the University Presses of Florida, Pensacola.

[58] *Documents of the American Revolution*, Volume 10.

Governor Galvez responded in kind by capturing several British vessels. The British complained and Galvez responded that they were taken only after the English war sloop *West Florida* seized Spanish vessels on Lake Pontchartrain.[59]

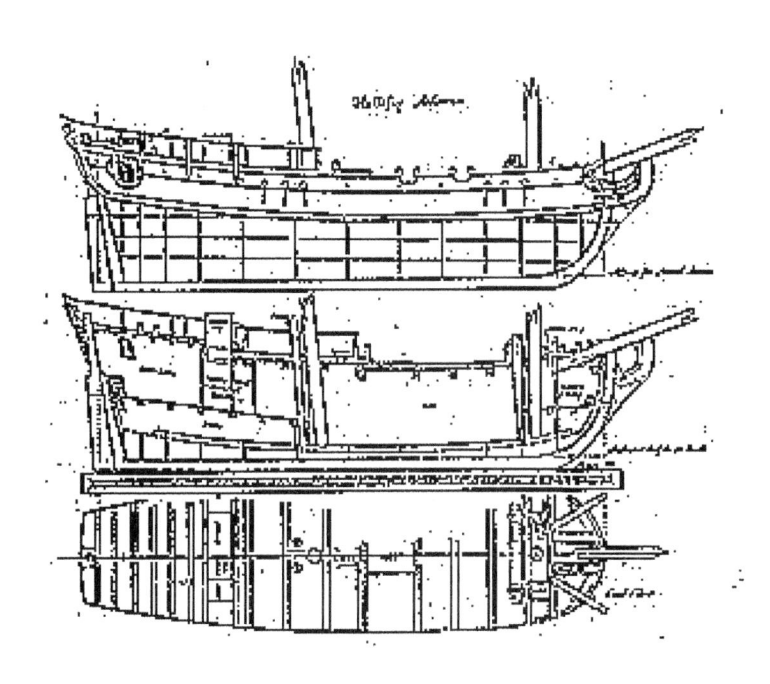

HMS *Hallifax* a Small schooner approximately the size of the *West Florida*

Before the war was declared the HMS *West Florida*, while assigned to patrol the Lakes leading to Manchac, had received permission from Spanish authorities to pass and repass

---

[59] *Documents of the American Revolution*, volume 9, page 823, letter from Governor Bernardo De Galvez to Governor Peter Chester at Pensacola August 26, 1777.

the Spanish Fort of St. John (at the entrance of bayou St. John off Lake Pontchartrain) without being stopped. Galvez rescinded that permission and Captain Burdon of the *West Florida* replied: "I will not suffer a boat to proceed across those Lakes or anywhere I may be cruising." In less than a week he had captured the two Spanish vessels mentioned above on Lake Pontchartrain.[60] Galvez then retaliated by capturing several British vessels.

By early 1778 there was a standoff on the Lakes with the British Navy in control outside of the range of Spanish coastal guns. The British were insisting they had the right to search all vessels and the Spanish just as vigorously contended the contrary. The commander of Fort St. John wrote to Governor Galvez on February 5, 1778: "My dear and most Venerated Lord: I have just news that a Garda Costa sloop of his Britannic Majesty mounting four guns and 25 to 30 men just entered Pontchartrain." The vessel was the *West Florida.* He asked what he should do if any of its officers asked to disembark or if in the immediate vicinity of the fort or under its guns the Captain presumes to examine vessels leaving the Bayou as happened the year before.[61]

Galvez replied that if any officers want to land to come into town (New Orleans) such was to be permitted provided they came and presented themselves to him. They were to be

---

[60] *Benardo De Galvez in Louisiana 1776 – 1783* by J. W. Caughey.

[61] *Documents of the American Revolution*, volume 11, page 296.

accompanied by a soldier from New Orleans. As to the examining of ships within reach of the forts cannon, the commander was to inform them with all prudence and politeness that they had no right to do so, if they persisted to inform Galvez so he could take whatever measures I think fit.[62] The Fort commander reported on March 22, 1778 that the *West Florida* was off Fort St. John stopping vessels and that he had advised the Captain that it was not proper to do so.[63]

The tension was growing. Soon after Galvez became Governor the British had taken an American schooner on Lake Pontchartrain which was considered by the Spanish to be Spanish territory. The Governor had retaliated by seizing all British ships between the Belize and Manchac on the Mississippi River. There were negotiations and some of the British ships were no doubt returned to their owners but from that time there was a cold war standoff between Spanish Louisiana and British West Florida.[64]

On January 14, 1778 Admiral Gayton had reported to the secretary of the Admiralty Philip Stephens "the two *Florida's* are on station."[65] But actually Captain Burden of the *West Florida*

---

[62] *Documents of the American Revolution*, volume 11, page 466, letter February 26, 1778.

[63] *Documents of the American Revolution*, volume 11, page 761.

[64] *Papers of the Continental Congress compiled 1774 – 1789*, record group 360.

[65] *Documents of the American Revolution*, volume 11; The survey schooner *Florida* had recently been converted to combat use by the addition of eight guns, Lieutenant Kirkland commanding, and

wrote on March 3, 1778 that he hoped to have the *Florida* sloop in the Lakes the following day.[66]

A vessel spending months on Pontchartrain, or for that matter any place along the northern Gulf Coast, quickly accumulates barnacles, oysters, toredo worm shells and green slime. Periodically bottom cleaning was done by careening at Pensacola. Commander Thomas Lloyd of HMS *Atlanta* at Pensacola reported to vice Admiral Gayton on January 18, 1778: "I have careen'd and sheathed HM sloop *West Florida* and the carpenter reports to me she will not run longer than six months except she gets a new bottom. I have given Mr. Burdon command with orders to proceed to the Lakes." [67]

On April 20, 1778 Commander Lloyd reported that the HMS *Florida* was also careened and the boat was unrepairable and was condemned.[68] Condemned vessels such as the *Florida* were scavenged for spare parts to maintain the other vessels.[69]

The cold war standoff on Lake Pontchartrain was about to grow hot. In January of 1778 Captain James Willing and his volunteer raiders left Fort Pitt on their armed boat the

---

was detached to Lake Ponchartrain and Maurepas. *The Economy of British West Florida*, page 149.

[66] *Documents of the American Revolution volume*, 11, page 698.

[67] *Documents of the American Revolution volume*, 11, page 156.

[68] *Documents of the American Revolution volume*, 11, page 157.

[69] *Log of HMS Mentor 1780-1781*, edited by James A. Servies, University Presses of Florida Pensacola.

Rattletrap for their raid on the Mississippi settlements and shipping in West Florida. The British were in the process of reinforcing their posts on the Mississippi River in response to Willing's raid when in June 1779 Spain declared war on England. The *West Florida* was then in a shooting war but first it had to survive the hurricane of August 18, 1779 which presumably she rode out somewhere on Lake Pontchartrain.

Small sloop similar to the *West Florida*

General Campbell likely did not know that he had received all the reinforcing troops that he was to receive from his commander, General Sir Henry Clinton. His war for West Florida with the Americans, French and Spanish was to be won or lost with the force that he had on hand. Although some vessels left the Pensacola station and some arrived they were few as a hurricane in October, 1780 inflicted much damage to the Jamaica squadron. By the time a small reinforcement arrived on 11 March 1781 it found a Spanish fleet outside Pensacola leaving the naval strength for the defense of Pensacola to HM vessels *Mentor* and *Port Royal* alone.[70]

The 14 gun brig – sloop HMS *Active* (launched 1776) had left Pensacola doing convoy escort and was captured by the American privateer *Gen. Pickering* off New York. The *Active* was replaced by HMS *Mentor* which arrived in Pensacola on May 14, 1780. The *Mentor* was an armed vessel with 24 guns captured from the Americans in 1778 and converted to the Liverpool privateer *Who's Afraid*. Sir Peter Parker purchased her at Jamaica in 1780 and renamed her *Mentor* and sent her off to Pensacola where she was later burned by her crew during the siege. The 14 gun HMS *Hound* (launched 1776) along with the store ship or ordnance vessel HMS *Earl of Bathurst* accompanied a convoy of merchant vessels from West Florida in the last week of February 1781.

The HMS *Earl of Bathurst* was a 385 – ton merchant vessel hired by the Ordnance Board, a government department under the Master General of Ordinance responsible for furnishing the Army and Navy with guns, ammunition and supplies. The ship was also used as a transport to overseas stations. The number of soldiers she carried was limited by the space needed for such stores and the large amounts of equipment for the garrisons of Florida took up much space. She was generally manned by a merchant crew of 18 men and four

---

[70] *The Economy of British West Florida 1763-1783* by Robin A. Fable.

boys under her Captain.[71] When the war with Spain commenced the *Earl of Bathurst* was armed at Pensacola as a warship. Her upgraded armament had been removed before she was lost to the Spanish.

The Sloop HMS *Stork* was purchased at Jamaica in 1777 and fitted out with 14 guns. In September 1779 she was damaged in a gale while trying to enter Pensacola harbor and in December was condemned as unseaworthy and sunk at Deer Point in Pensacola harbor as a careening hulk.[72] HMS *Port Royal* was an 18 gun sloop, formerly the French armed merchant vessel *Comte de Maurepas* which was captured by the British in 1778. They armed her with 18 six pounder guns and gave her the name *Port Royal*. She was captured by the Spanish at Pensacola in 1781.

When the advanced redoubt at Pensacola was exploded during the siege which led to the capitulation of Pensacola in 1781, 40 seamen from the *Mentor* and *Port Royal* were killed.[73]

---

[71] *A Royal American: A New Jersey Officer in the Kings Service during the Revolution* by John Frederick.

[72] *Archaeology of Colonial Pensacola* by Judith Ann Bense, University of Florida press. The Stork is known as the Deadman's Island shipwreck.

[73] *Major Robert Farmar's Journal of the Siege of Pensacola*, *The Historical Magazine and Notes and Queries Concerning the Antiquties and Biography of America*, Vol. IV, pages 166-172, New York 1860.

The Spanish Naval Situation

By the time Galvez arrived off Pensacola in 1781 he had four small vessels from New Orleans under his direct command and a fleet from Havana that included a 74 gun ship of the line. Such was not the case in 1779 when Spain declared war. Galvez needed what few vessels he had for his expedition up the Mississippi River. He had a problem in that the British sloop *West Florida* controlled Lake Pontchartrain and access to Manchac. There was no direct ship access from Lake Pontchartrain to the Mississippi River but access by a short wagon road portage from Manchac to the river.[74]

Fortunately Galvez also had a potential solution to his problem. The American vessel *Morris* under Captain William Pickles had recently been sunk by hurricane in the Mississippi River below New Orleans. Forty-five of her crew of fifty-six had survived the hurricane and many of those were immediately available. The solution then was to provide Oliver Pollock with a ship for Pickles and his crew and ask Pollock to send it into the Lake to confront the *West Florida*. Available was the *Caindre,* a large armed schooner which Galvez made available to Pollock.

---

[74] The D'Iberville River now called Bayou Manchac flowed from the Mississippi east to Lake Pontichatrian in times of river flooding. At normal stages the several hundred yards adjacent to the Mississippi was not navigatable. All navigation was cut off when the Corps of Engineers built the present levees.

Pollock took on the challenge. He took possession of the *Caindre*, outfitting her as needed and placed aboard the surviving crew of the *Morris* with Pickles as captain and Pierre Rousseau as chief officer. She was never commissioned as a Continental vessel and is often referred to as the *Morris* or the *Morris's Tender* although there is no documentation of her having been renamed as such. She could well have been a tender for the *Morris* which was outfitting on the River several miles below New Orleans when struck by the hurricane. Such and outfitting would have required one or more tenders.[75] Previously quoted was a report from General Campbell of a large schooner entering the Lake which, in his opinion, put the vessel *West Florida* at risk. That vessel was the *Caindre* under Captain Pickles looking for a fight.

The name Of Captain Pickles vessel in which he captured the *West Florida* on September 10, 1779 has been the subject of much speculation by historians over the years. I refer to her as the *Caindre* because that is the name given by her chief officer Pierre Rousseau in his after-action report to the Spanish authorities in New Orleans dated September 12, 1779.

The Dictionary of American Naval Fighting Ships, an Internet publication by The Navy Historical Center of the Department of the Navy, says she was "the Continental armed schooner *Morris*". Howard I. Chapelle in *The History of the American sailing Navy* at page 96 states that the ship *Morris*,

---

[75] In the final fitting out of a naval vessel before a voyage it was good to get some distance away from the port with its many distractions for the crew.

sank in a hurricane, was replaced by a schooner of the same name, presented by some citizens residing in the Spanish colony of Louisiana.

Charles Oscar Paullin in his *Navy of the American Revolution* says only that Galvez "spared" Pollock an armed schooner. The internet encyclopedia *Wikipedia* as of March 14, 2013 listed the USS *Morris* as a schooner in the Continental Navy placed in commission in 1779, stating that the *Morris* was presented to Oliver Pollock by Governor Galvez in the summer of 1779 for the use of American forces on the Mississippi River. Another Internet publication titled *Louisiana's Military Heritage* published by the USS Kidd Veterans Memorial called the vessel the *Morris*. Caughey in his *Bernardo De Galvez in Louisiana 1776 – 1783* states at page 72 that Captain Pickle's vessel was: "the American privateer known as the corvette of the '*Morris*' (formally the *Rebecca*)." In the *Journals of the Continental Congress 1774 – 1787*, volume 17, page 1130 it is stated that the *West Florida* British sloop of war was captured by the Continental schooner ship "*Morris's Tender*" under the command of William Pickles. In volume 17 page 60 Congress refers to the vessel simply as "a schooner in the service of the United States". First officer Rousseau and his after action report refers to the vessel as "the schooner *Caindre* of the frigate *Morris*".

The *Caindre* was only "made available" or loaned by Galvez and/or some citizens of New Orleans and was never owned by Pollock or the United States. Pollock in a letter to Congress stated: "it was his intention to get a schooner for

Captain Pickles to cruise in."[76] Pollock never commissioned her into the United States Navy. Thus it is highly unlikely that he would have or could have changed her name given the probable requirements of title or ownership by the Spanish equivalent of a Coast Guard Registrar of Vessels. We can reasonably assume from the above references that the *Caindre* had been serving as a tender to the *Morris* as she was being fitted out in the river below New Orleans prior to her encounter with the hurricane and Rousseau references her to the *Morris*.

---

[76] *Papers of the Continental Congress Compiled 1774 – 1789*, record group 360.

The Battle on Lake Pontchartrain

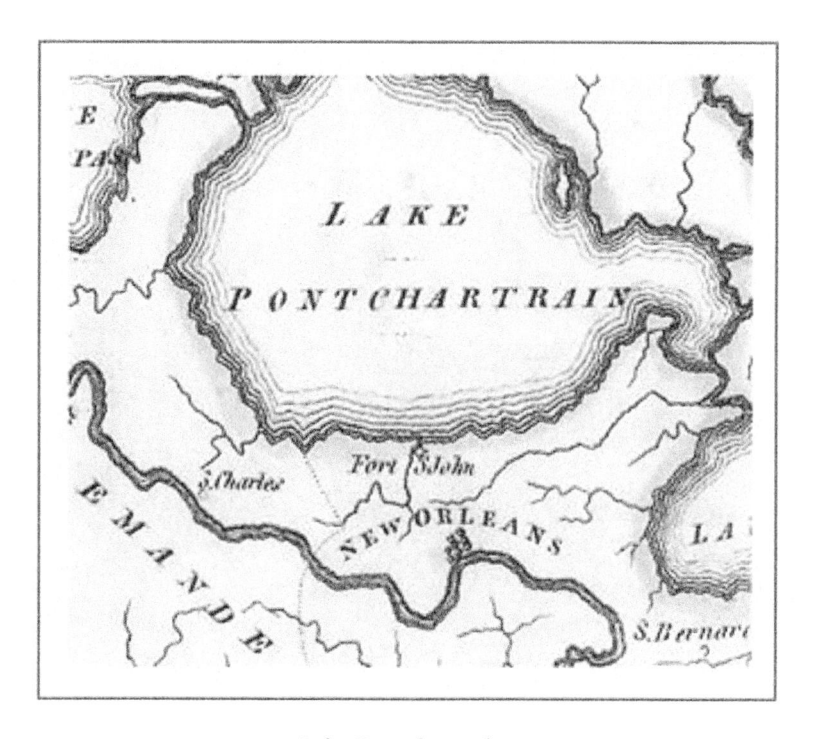

Lake Pontchartrain

In Early September 1779 HMS *West Florida* was cruising on Lake Pontchartrain. We do not know her exact location on the Lake, nor is it of great consequence although she was within swimming distance of shore or at least swimming distance of one of the participants of the upcoming battle who did so. Her Captain and crew were not aware that Spain had entered the ongoing war between England and France nor were they aware that a hostile vessel had entered the Lake. She was on a remote, disagreeable station with unreliable mails.

Rather than summarize, paraphrase of place in my own words the description of the battle I shall simply quote, or quote translations of the after-action reports of the participants in the battle between the American *Caindre*, sometimes referred to as the *Morris* or the *Morris's Tender* and the British *West Florida*, but first, to give you a feeling of the situation and the difficulty of communications I quote a letter dated December 20, 1779 from Captain LeMontais of HMS *Stork* then at Pensacola to Vice Admiral Sir Peter Parker in Jamaica:

"*Stork* Pensacola December 20, 1779

"Sir:

"I take the earliest opportunity of acknowledging the receipt of your letter by the *Carteral* packet which arrived the 8th September enclosing orders for commencing hostilities with Spain; and also your favor of 25th October by the *Earl Bathurst* store ship by which I am concerned to find you have not received any of my letters viz one dated 6 April by the *Diligence*

Packet and one by Mr. Henderson who was bound on a schooner to Montego Bay dated 6 July as likewise by the *Comet* Packet in duplicate of that sent the 6 July representing the very bad condition of his Majesty's Sloop *Stork* under my command, which we experienced so much in a late voyage to Mobile where we have been by request of Maj. Gen. Campbell during which we found her so very leaky that on my arrival here the 10th instant I thought it necessary for my own justification as it was the opinion of my officers that she was not in condition to go to sea again, to call a survey on her hull, and for that purpose there was not any of his Majesty's ships here, I thought it proper to call on Lieutenant Emery commanding the *Earl Bathurst*, and Lieutenant Arthur Clarke now in the service of the post office together with the most experience ship carpenters in this place to attend the survey as will appear by the enclosed order and report; and they having deemed her entirely unfit for service I propose continuing her afloat with the officers people and stores on board as long as she will float which is very doubtful, until I shall receive your orders how to dispose of them; but if she should prove so leaky as not to be able to keep her above the water or should she go on shore from the badness of _____[77] which I have long expected, and there are not any to be purchased in this place, in such case I propose returning the gunners stores to the ordnance storekeeper here, and make tents on shore for people and other stores, there being nobody to receive them.

---

[77] Indecipherable partial word but possibly referring to anchors or rodes.

"As both myself and officers have long been out of England and a considerable time on this disagreeable employment where there is no field for acquiring either credit or promotion we are earnestly desirous of going to England as soon as possible and strenuously entreat your permission for that purpose so we may avail ourselves of the spring convoy or the first favorable opportunity that may offer.

"In respect to the hull of the vessel I have to mention that I conceive she might be serviceably employed to be sunk at Deer Point as a careening hulk for small vessels on this station.

"I am extremely sorry to inform you of the loss of the Mississippi and the western parts of this province Col. Dixon having been obliged to surrender to a much superior force of the enemy on the terms of the enclosed capitulation; and it is my concern to acquaint you at the same time of the loss of the *Florida*[78] armed sloop and I most sincerely regret the loss of so good an officer as the commander Lieutenant John Payne who from his knowledge of this coast must be and a special loss to the service; since you will see the particulars by the enclosed letter, and therefore shall only add that the gallant defense he made does honor to his country: I think it is also necessary to mention that upon application from General Campbell immediately after the arrival of the packet I sent eight men in a boat with an express to Col. Dixon and Lieutenant Payne to inform them of the Spanish War which all fell into the enemy's hands.

---

[78] The *West Florida*.

"I have the honor to be with great respect Sir, Your most obedient and most humble servant. LeMontais" [79]

The Captain LeMontais letter illustrates why the Pensacola station was considered to be a hardship post. The commander of the fourteen gun *Stork* was sending reports, advising the western part of the province and other captains of the war with Spain and trying to maintain his vessel without the resources to do so. In addition, during that period every ship on the horizon was a potential enemy as the naval war was on its way to West Florida.

Captain Pickles and the *Caindre* [80] had sailed out the mouth of the Mississippi then northeastwardly along the Chandelier Islands to Lake Borgne then west through the Rigolets and into Lake Pontchartrain where the *West Florida* was soon sighted.

The capture of the HMS *West Florida* is reported by Gulf Coast historians and in naval histories of the Revolution. What has been missing from the histories of the battle are the details available only from the actual reports of the participants. The American and British eyewitness after-action reports paint very different pictures as to the strength and readiness of the combatants. Lieutenant Payne, the Captain of the *West Florida* was killed in the battle and a report by Captain Pickles has not

---

[79] Public Record Office, London, Admiralty 1/ 242 folio 456, Admirals Dispatches from Stations in Jamaica, dispatch dated 7 April 1780 by Sir Peter Parker.
[80] "Caindre" is an old French word loosely meaning fear or dread.

been located. The report of Masters Mate Savage survived in a very readable form. Unfortunately Lieutenant Rousseau's report found in the Spanish archives was in poor condition, was replete with misspellings and the copying of the bound report deleted several characters from the right margin of the pages.

First office Pierre George Rousseau gave his after action report, in French, two days after the battle at Fort St. John. There were two letters or reports from participants on the British side.

First officer Rousseau was an experienced mariner/ship captain who had distinguished himself as a commander of a privateer during the early days of the Revolution. He was born in France in 1751. His mother died young and he immigrated to Virginia or South Carolina with his merchant ship owner/captain father as a child. He was in New Orleans by 1764. In 1775 he was commissioned as an officer of the Continental Navy. In 1779 Oliver Pollock appointed him as first Lieutenant of the Continental vessel Morris. Pollock advised Congress: he (Rousseau) "was commander of one of your cruisers out of Cape Francois[81] and this taken made a most gallant defense and consequence of which I have appointed him first Lieutenant of the Morris." Pollock stated that he and Captain Pickles were pleased with all the officers.

We do not have the names of any the other officers and crew of the *Morris* or the *West Florida* except for seaman Brown

---

[81] A port in Saint-Domingue which is present day Cap-Haitien, Haiti.

of the *Caindre* who was named in a cover letter that accompanied Rousseau's report as a traitor: "who sought to prevent the crew from fighting [the West Florida] their defect being that the battery was strong and that they would be cut in pieces and that their defeat was inevitable". Another report simply refers to the crewmen as: "Brown traitor to our cause swimed ashore".[82]

After the capture of the *West Florida* Rousseau was for a short period of time given command of her as prize captain following which he entered Spanish service as a brevet Lieutenant of militia.

The records of the Louisiana Infantry Regiment[83] and the Louisiana Militia Companies show that Pedro Russo, being one and the same as Pierre Georges Rousseau, was made a Captain of Louisiana militia on January 1, 1780[84] and was made captain of the army in 1784. He served the King of Spain faithfully for 24 years and in 1791 was appointed the first

---

[82] *Bernado de Galvez in Louisiana 1776 – 1783* by J. W. Caughey, page 72.
[83] *Honor and Fidelity* by Jack D. L. Holmes a part of the Louisiana Collection Series.
[84] Jack D. L. Holmes in his forward to the book *Rousseau: The Last Days of Spanish New Orleans* by Martinez says that Governor Galvez at a point in time shortly after the capture of the *West Florida* recommended Rousseau for a breveted lieutenancy and command of the Brigantine Corsair *Galvez – Town*, page III.

commander of the Spanish squadron of galleys on the Mississippi River following the revolutionary war.[85]

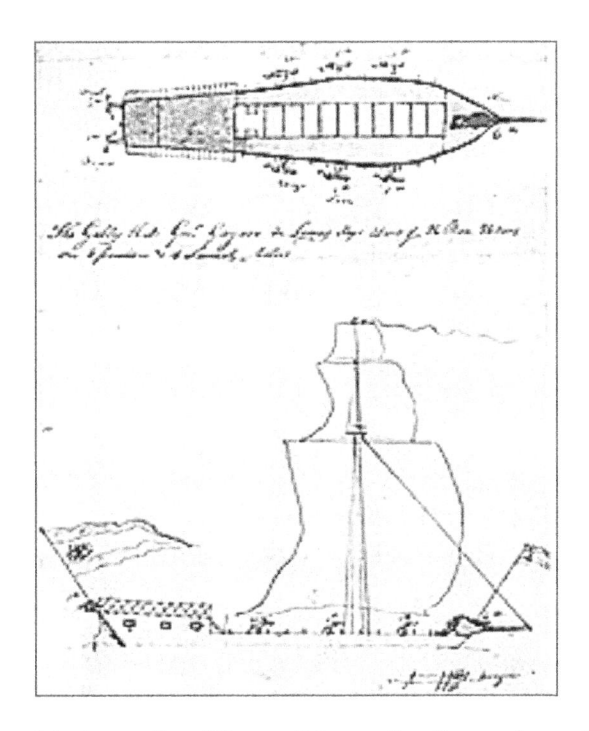

Spanish river galley, 28 men, 24 oars, One 6 pounder and six swivils.

The Louisiana militia encompassed land and naval service. Rousseau was in command of the Brigantine *Galvez* or *Galveztown* at the siege of Mobile in 1780 and was captain of that vessel at Pensacola in 1781 when General Galvez came on board and made his famous dash past the batteries at the harbor entrance. In 1784 Rousseau was placed in command of

---

[85] *Spanish War Vessels on the Mississippi, 1792 – 1796* by Abraham P. Nasatir, Yale University press, 1968, page 32.

the Northwestern Louisiana post of Nacogdoches, situated on the Red River.

The Rousseau after action report with its cover letter was located in Spain and translated for the author in 1988 by Mobile historian and author Jay Higginbotham. Jay's comments on the translation were: "I have done the best that I can. Much of it is illegible. Some of the words are misspelled. The word Enfante, which I have underlined with a red pencil, means children. It's a complete mystery to me what children were doing in a naval battle."

The following is the translation of the Rousseau after-action report including blank spaces representing the several untranslatable words:

"Account of the combat of the schooner *Caindre* of the frigate Morris, Captain William Pickler, American, against the boat, *West Florida*, of Pensacola, Captain Paine.

"Having arrived on the lake on the 10th of this month at one o'clock in the afternoon, we got together first with the vessel, *West Florida*, and we approached it, he also closed on us. Our Captain Pickles has caused _____ bar and caused all of the people at his station and _____ _____, near _____ according to his order, he ordered Lieutenant Russo to keep himself in front ready to show at the boarding after the musketry and the firing of the rock guns; then to go beyond the wind and run next to the boat. After having talked with him and asking him who he was, he said he was the *West Florida*, he in turn asks us where we came from: _____ after having responded that we came from the same neighborhood, he said he was quite satisfied. At which Captain Pickles told him that he would repent soon and on the hour having brought the English flag down and hoisted the American flag; as soon as the combat started and very_____, the two captains, and after the first burst, having boarded by the rear the starboard, the Captain took aboard my children,[86] the Lieutenant Rousseau, a sergeant and three others wished to mount, were repulsed by the blow of lances up to their deck; sir Rousseau going back to the stern, he being only slightly wounded in the hand, seeing his Captain who boarded at aft the deck, following him as well, the said sir having mounted by the quarter deck, the Captain with him, and all of the people having followed him, they made themselves masters. Found the Captain of the boat wounded to death at their feet with three other men, and the rest on the bridge and who demanded good quarter and who throw themselves in _____ in the hold. Captain Pickles and Sir Rousseau made their efforts for reducing the fury of their people on those who asked them for quarter, which was given them at once. Captain Pickles finding himself master of the boat made Lieutenant Rousseau the master of the boat.

"The said boat was armed with two cannons of six and two of four ____ _____ of _____ with a rail or bulwark surrounding of 9 1/2 inch thickness and 10 small swivel guns mounted on pivots on top of the rail or bulwark which make them dominate on _____ _____ a considerable advantage; furthermore they had some lances, ___ axes, and many other utensils of war. The number of men which they had aboard was

---

[86] There were six cabin boys on board as part of the crew.

28 or 30 among which were found several Americans who they had forced to serve.

"The schooner of Captain Pickles was armed only with four little cannons of 2 1/2 pounds of balls and another of 1 1/2 pound with ten small swivels on _____ without any bulwarks or lockers and everybody was in the open, of the fashion that of the boat one would see the equipment from head to foot; it's crew was in number from 51 _____ and six cabin boys, of which there had been killed three of the crew. From the Fort St. John on 12 September 1779.

"Pierre Rousseau (superior?) American Lieutenant"[87]

The battle is described from the British point of view by letter dated October 24, 1779 to Captain LeMontais from Mr. Jerrald Savage who was master's mate of the *West Florida* during the battle:

"Sir:

"It is with the greatest concern I acquaint you of the loss of worthy good officer and a sincere friend Lieutenant John Payne who deservedly lamented fell on the 10th day of September last in an engagement between his Majesty's armed sloop the *West Florida* which he commanded and an American privateer In the Lake Pontchartrain. An abstract of the particulars (as in duty) I transmit you.

---

[87] Archivo General de Indias, Sevilla, Spain, in the section Papeles de Cuba, file 192.

"On the aforesaid date at noon weigh'd for Pensacola, giving up hopes of seeing a yard boat dispatched with an officer and seven men express to Col. Dixon at Manchac the 29th ult. at 2:00 p.m. on the said 10th. Saw a sail and gave chase came up and hailed she answered from Pensacola to Manchac at the same time grappled on the starboard quarter and began to engage; attempted boarding twice but repulsed, in the third was boarded by a large body in which Mr. Payne received a mortal wound of which he died some small time after and the sloop unfortunately carried, I received some slight wounds of which I am perfectly recovered. The privateer mounted eight guns – 65 men – Pickles commander. From sending the note to Manchac (which was taken the same day she went) and which reduced our numbers to 15 some of those sickly as also stripping the starboard breastwork the day before engagement laid us at every disadvantage.

"In justice to the officers in whose hands fate has thrown us; have behaved with great humanity, from the best authority I have the number killed, belonging to the privateer is 8, the wounded I cannot ascertain, on the side of his Majesty, one officer and one private killed, eight prisoners from the present situation of affairs I do not wish to dwell father on the subject. Mr. Pollock, agent for the congress, has informed me he will write to the commander in chief at Pensacola acquainting him; if there be any American prisoners there, he would wish a cartel might take place. I am with sincere respect, your most obedient humble servant, Jerrald Savage."[88]

---

[88] Public Record Office, London, Referance Adm. 242

Notwithstanding the translation problems, the after-action reports present a fairly clear picture of the Pontchartrain battle. Clearly Captain Pickles had the advantage of surprise. The ruse of using the British flag to close, pulling down that flag and simultaneously firing and raising your own flag employed by Pickles was commonly used and should not have deceived anyone. Lieutenant Payne was in the middle of a high tension cold war conflict between Britain and Spain and was at war with France and the rebelling Colonies. Even though he was unaware that war with Spain had actually been declared the situation required him to stay alert and treat every approaching ship as if it were an enemy until there was positive identification to the contrary. Prudence should have required him upon sighting the unknown *Caindre* to call his crew to quarters, run out his guns and for the gunners to have their matches ready to fire on a moment's notice.

Captain Pickles had been at war with Britain for several years and was on a mission to take the *West Florida* which was likely known to be the only other vessel on the Lake. He used the common ruse of flying the British flag and being an Englishman he was able to respond convincingly to Lieutenant Payne's challenge.

The *Caindre* was a vessel with open deck, no fore or poop decks and thus no place to hide the large armed crew with their muskets. It was common in such circumstances to attempt to disguise the crew to look like friendly merchant seamen. During that period merchant crewmen and man-of-war crewmen, except for certain special occasions, dressed much the same. Pickles and his officers and marines were probably dressed in something other than Continental naval uniforms which were mostly left to the whim of the captain and likely not available in New Orleans in any event.[89] The crew of the *Caindre* would have had their assigned arms and stations and since the plan was to close and board his guns and pivots would have been loaded and ready to fire with their anti-personnel projectiles.

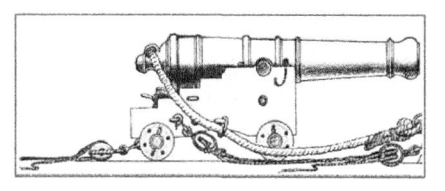

Carriage Gun

The ruse worked and Lieutenant Payne allowed Pickles to close, fire his guns and muskets, secure his vessel alongside with grapnels and, admittedly at great risk and loss of life, to board his vessel. Boarding reduced the battle to hand-to-hand combat with swords, pikes, pistols, knives, axes, fists and teeth. Yes, it was that kind of battle. "Brown traitor to our cause [who] swimed ashore" was correct in that in a long-range artillery duel the *Caindre* would probably have been overpowered because the guns of the *West Florida* were substantially heavier and her heavy bulwarks would have further reduced the effectiveness of Pickles four 2 1/2 – pounder guns.

According to Rousseau the *West Florida* had high bulwarks some 9 ½ inches thick and was armed with two 6-pounder cannons, two 4 ½-pounder cannons, and 10 swivels on top of the tall bulwarks "at a height to dominate". The six pounders and 4 1/2 pounders would have been mounted on

---

[89] When I was in the ninth grade I read the entire *Horatio Hornblower* series of books which led me on a lifelong study of sailing ships, navies and battles. Some of this discussion is conjecture but I think plausible conjecture.

four truck or wheeled carriages and fired through ports. The swivels are small cannons that would fire a ball of 1/2 to 1 1/2 pounds. The "bastingaige of siege" is interpreted by Caughey[90] as a 9 1/2 pounder cannon. I interpret "a bastingaige of siege of 9 1/2 inches" to be a rail or bulwark. Jay Higginbotham did not attempt to translate the word.

This would have meant the *West Florida* had a broadside weight[91] of 10 1/2 pounds plus the swivels.

From the reports Captain Payne was hailing Pickles and closed or allowed Pickles to close on his starboard quarter. Grappling hooks were thrown and secured and the ships were pulled together as the Americans opened fire with their cannons, rock guns and small arms. Unfortunately for the British the previous day Payne had removed all or part of the barricade on the starboard side of the ship which partially opened it to small arms fire.[92]

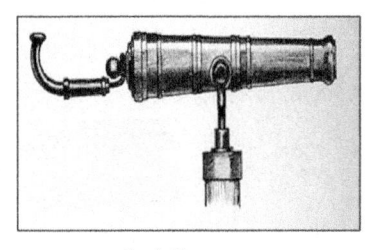

The *Caindre* was armed, according to Rousseau, with four 2 1/2 pounder truck guns, perhaps one 1 1/2 pounder, probably a swivel, and ten swivels only

Swivil gun

---

[90] J. W. Caughey, *Bernardo De Galvez and Louisiana 1776 – 1783*.

[91] Broadside weight is the total weight of shot fired in one volley (broadside) from the guns on one side of the vessel not including swivels which are small short range weapons.

[92] *George Gauld; Surveyor and Cartographer of the Gulf Coast* by John D. Ware, revised and completed by Robert R. Ray, University Presses of Florida.

described as "small" giving for the *Caindre* a broadside weight of 5 pounds plus the swivels. The weight of shot per broadside of the British guns were more than double that of the Americans. According to Rousseau the ammunition used for the first fire of the swivel guns was rocks, a close range anti-personnel load.

Caughey quoted a Spanish report regarding Pickles capture of the *West Florida* as: "It is unbelievable that he should have captured it on account of the disparity in size of the ships, their armaments, etc."

We have no means of determining with precision the relative size of the vessels. In various reports the *West Florida* is referred to as a British frigate, a sloop or a sloop of war. Congress called her a sloop of war and Galvez referred to her while in American service as a privateer. None of those terms are helpful in determining the size of a vessel. During The Revolutionary war naval "sloops" were vessels with guns on one deck without regard to rig. During that period vessels classed as sloops, had one or two masts, and carried from 8 to 18 guns. The sloop classification changed from time to time and by the last quarter of the century a "sloop of war" came to mean a vessel commanded by an officer one grade below a Captain in the Navy with her main armament on one deck. Ship rigged sloops of war, such as the HMS *Hermes* sunk off Fort Boyer in 1815 (now the location of Fort Morgan), did not become a standard class until about the end of the American Revolution.

We do know from information provided by Admiral Gayton the that the *West Florida* was of 60 tons with a 6 foot draft aft which would indicate a vessel between 40 and 60 feet in length. The *Caindre,* although described as being a large schooner, is stated in the Spanish reports to be substantially smaller than her opponent. Her open deck with no fore or poop decks gave her a substantial height disadvantage in a boarding fight.

Pollock reported to Congress only that Captain Pickles had sailed on a cruise in August and captured in September "a vessel of very superior force in Lake Pontchartrain after a very severe conflict."[93]

Captain Pickles did have a larger crew. Rousseau says he had a crew of 51 which apparently do not include the 6 cabin boys while the *West Florida* had aboard 28 or 30 among which were several Americans "forced to serve."[94] The British account was different stating that the *West Florida* had a crew of 15 and that her starboard breastwork or boarding netting had been removed the day before. The report also said that the *Caindre* had a crew of 65 men.

In a long-range artillery duel the greater numbers of crew would have been of no benefit while out ranged with larger guns. Certainly in a boarding fight the larger crew was an advantage but then the British had a height advantage defending their higher bulwarks with their pikes.

---

[93] *Papers of the Continental Congress* compiled 1774 – 1789, record group 360.
[94] The British Navy fought and won most of its battles with a combination of volunteer and pressed seamen.

Notwithstanding, the Americans prevailed. Captain Pickles and his party first attempted to board aft starboard amidships but were repulsed. Rousseau, Pickles and the crew successfully boarded by the stern, took the quarter deck and drove the surrendering crew below decks. Or, the British version is that after grappling to the starboard side Pickles attempted to board twice, was repelled but succeeded the third time. In any event it was a quick bloody hard fought battle.

Cruising the Lake

After the battle the *West Florida* put in at Fort St. John on the south shore of Lake Pontchartrain where Rousseau's after-action report was prepared. I have found no records relating to the *Caindre* following the battle. Captain Pickles stayed on the Lake with the *West Florida* for a period of time. Lieutenant Rousseau may have taken the *Caindre* back to the Mississippi River and returned her to Governor Galvez as he entered Spanish service immediately following the battle.

Following her capture Pollock inquired of Galvez if keeping the West Florida cruising the Lake would be useful to the common cause or if she should be sent home in place of the Morris. Galvez replied as follows: "as I have actually no craft with which to substitute in the lakes the privateer, 'West Florida,' I ask you, that, notwithstanding the orders you have received from the honorable Congress, and, provided always, that you should derive no prejudiced from your action, to issue orders, as well for the security of this colony as for the welfare of the 'common cause,' to the effect the said privateer shall remain in the lakes until I shall be able to send another in her stead.

"I herewith annex, conformable with your request, the report of the expedition which you have witnessed against the British settlements on the River.

"God grant you long life, Bernardo De Galvez, New Orleans, October 21, 1779." [95]

On September 26, 1776 Pickles was cruising the Lake with the *West Florida*. He transported 122 Indians across the Lake to New Orleans, by way of Bayou St. John, and the following day took a prize on the Mobile coast with 13 Negroes aboard valued at $2660.

In addition to providing a defense against British naval incursions into Lake Pontchartrain and preventing the transportation of troops for a counterattack to retake Baton Rouge or Natchez Captain Pickles in the *West Florida* secured the submission of the inhabitants of the north shore of Lake Pontchartrain to the United States. The area was settled largely by Tory sympathizers many of which had fled from the war in the seaboard states. Unfortunately many were also still upset

---

[95] *Mississippi as a Province, Territory and State* by J.F.H. Claiborne, volume 1, page 122, published Jackson Mississippi 1880. Pollock reported to Congress that Galvez urged him to continue the cruise on the lakes for the protection of trade which he did until the month of January 1780 when the *West Florida* under Pickles proceeded to the rendezvous of the force about to go against Mobile and Pensacola. *Papers of the Continental Congress compiled 1774 – 1789*, record group 360.

over the treatment by Captain Willing's raiders so a diplomatic touch was required.

It was reported In the *Journals of the Continental Congress*, volume 17, page 600, after referring to letters from Governor Galvez and Oliver Pollock, that in September 1779 Captain William Pickles commanding a schooner in the services of the United States entered Lake Pontchartrain and captured the British armed sloop *West Florida* which had been in possession and command of the Lake for the previous two years, and after taking the sloop landed part of his men in the district or country of Lake Pontchartrain between the Bayou le Combe and the River Tanchipano and obtained from the inhabitants of that district a submission in writing. The committee further noted that according to the letters of Governor Galvez, Captain Pickles and the sloop *West Florida* by joining the forces of the States under his command with that of Spain greatly facilitated the reduction of West Florida which may, in the opinion of the committee, have served to strengthen and support the claim of the United States to the free navigation of the River Mississippi and to a port or ports on the said River. The committee further noted that Pickles actions gave the Continental Congress additional claims by capture to territory in West Florida.[96] A memorandum to that effect was forwarded to John Jay, Ambassador to Spain.

---

[96] *The Siege of Mobile, 1780, in Maps* by William S. Coker and Hazel P. Coker contained in *Alabama and the Borderlands from Prehistory to Statehood*, University of Alabama Press.

The submission agreement signed by the north shore inhabitants states: "*** the said William Pickles, Esq., did on the twenty-first of the same month land some of his people and take possession of the settlement and gave us all the protection against Indians and others that his force would admit of; and suffered us to remain on our possession till further orders. We therefore consider ourselves belonging to the said States and are willing to remain here and enjoy our property and privileges under the said United States. October 16, 1779."[97]

Ohio River row galley with removable bulwarks - 1782

---

[97] *The Geoffigons and the Revolution* an Internet family history site by a descendent whose Geoffigon ancestor signed the submission agreement.

The Continental Sloop *West Florida* at Mobile

After about a month on the lakes the *West Florida* sailed to New Orleans where, at the request of Oliver Pollock, as Continental agent, and Captain Pickles, acting also as agent for the crew, the vessel, her guns and all articles aboard were inventoried and appraised for 2700 Spanish milled dollars. This was the age were crews were incentivized by prize money. Pollock took the sloop at the valuation for the use of the United States and gave a certificate to the captors which was in due course honored and the dollars divided among the crew in a formula that greatly favored the captain and officers.[98]

During January 1780 the newly commissioned Continental naval vessel *West Florida* was completely fitted out by Pollock and armed with four 6-pounder cannon and 12 swivel guns. On 20 January Pollock appointed Captain Pickles to command the vessel. She was provisioned for 60 days with a crew of 58. Pickles was directed to proceed to Ship Island to join the Spanish fleet already in route to Mobile.

---

[98] *Journals of the Continental Congress 1774 – 1789*, volume 18, page 1130.

The Spanish fleet at Mobile Bay March 1780

Pickles was to assist Galvez in the campaigns against Mobile and Pensacola for 20 days or longer if necessary. After he completed that assignment, Pickles was to go to Havana for a cargo of tafia[99] and sugar (for use by the Continental Army), then convey it to Philadelphia — or some other port that was safe from the enemy.[100]

General Galvez embarked for Mobile at New Orleans on January 11, 1780. According to his journal his convoy consisted of one merchant frigate, four fettees, a packet boat, two brigantines, the 20 gun Kings frigate *Volante*, the galliot *Venezuela*, the privateer brig *Galvez* and the Kings brig *Koulician*. Caughey describes the *"brig Galvez"* as a privately armed corsair (privateer).[101]

The fleet sailed on January 14th and on the 16th crossed the bar at the mouth of the Mississippi River.[102] Upon entering the Gulf the fleet of 12 vessels encountered a storm which caused the loss of some of the vessels but no loss of life. To repair the battered ships and awaiting reinforcements they anchored on the 18th at Southeast Pass of the Mississippi and

---

[99] Tafia was a molasses-based rum popular at the time. It was flammable and on British warships was frequently stored in large casks in the hold of the vessels. Several ships were lost to tafia fires.

[100] *Alabama and the Borderlands* by William S. Coker and Hazel P. Coker, page 17.

[101] *Bernardo De Galvez in Louisiana 1776 – 1783* by John Walton Caughey, page 175.

[102] *Journal of Don Bernardo de Galvez,* Mobile, March 20, 1780.

on the February 28, 1780 sailed from East Pass. On 7 February Galvez went aboard "his brig" the *Galvez*. On February 8 the fleet was off the Perdido River and on the 9th was off Mobile Bar.

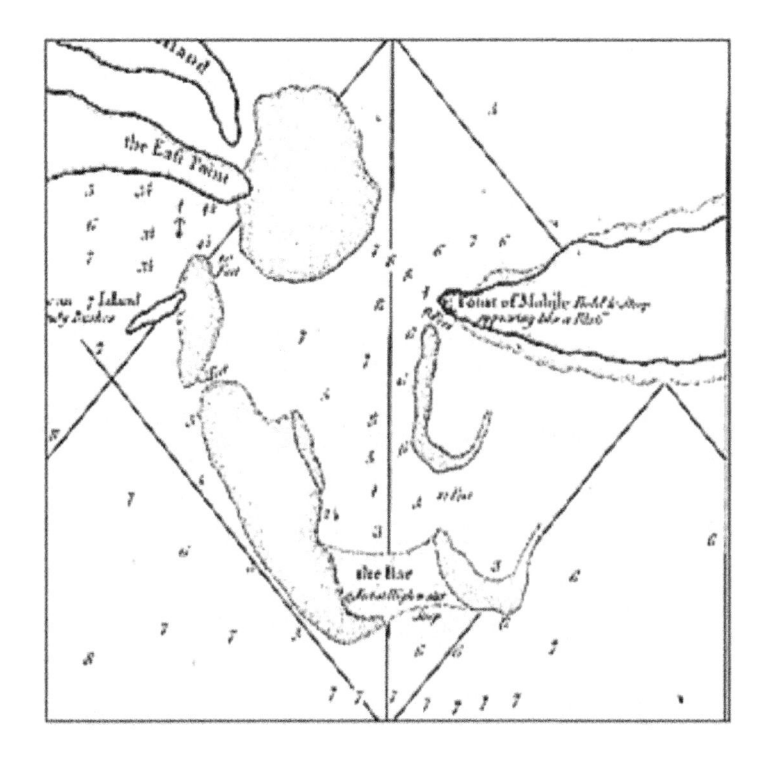

Entrance to Mobile Bay - 1794

As the fleet approached the entrance to Mobile Bay they took the British supply vessel *Brownhall*. The loss of the *Brownhall* was a blow to the British as it was carrying to Mobile presents brought by the ordnance ship *Earl of Bathurst* for a proposed Indian conference scheduled to be held at Mobile.[103]

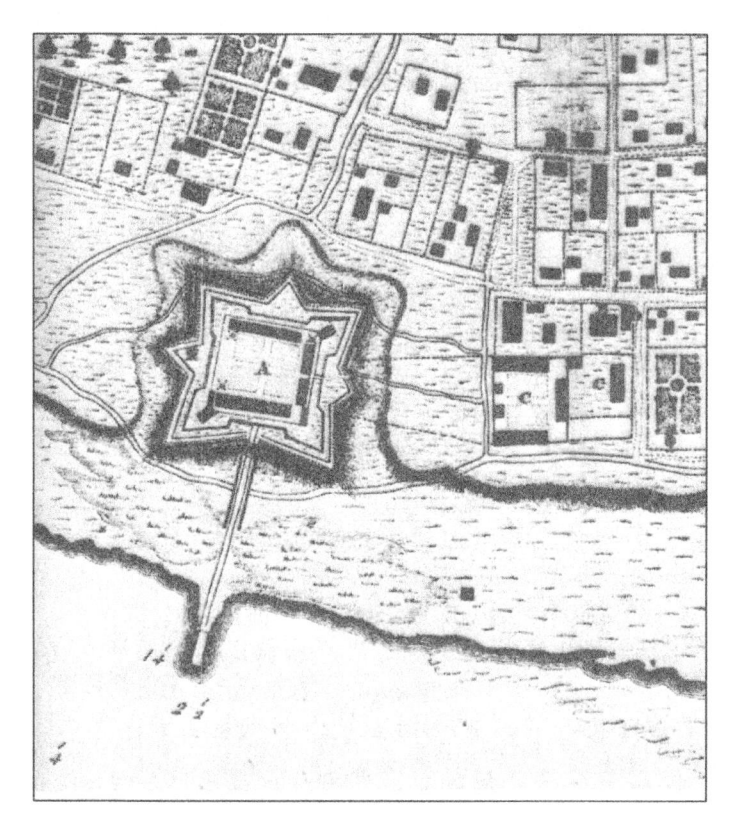

British Fort Charlotte

Another account is given in a Letter to Congress from Oliver Pollock dated April 26, 1780.[104] Pollock states that he was present when General Galvez sailed from New Orleans about 1

---

[103] Peter Joseph Hamilton, *Colonial Mobile*, page 313.
[104] *Papers of the Continental Congress, compiled 1774 – 1789*, record group 360.

February. His fleet and army consisted of a 20 gun ship, two 14 or 16 gun brigs, ten polacres or other vessels mounting cannon together with 700 troops and 800 militia along with all the necessary equipment and supplies that could be secured at New Orleans to besiege Pensacola or Mobile. They expected to be joined at the mouth of the Mississippi River by a fleet from Havana carrying troops but were disappointed so they moved back into the mouth of the river, anchored up and waited.

The expected reinforcement fleet arrived on March 4 whereupon they sailed for Mobile Bay. On 6 March a very heavy gale cast the frigate *Volante* of 20 guns, a snow, a brig and a polacre on the middle ground between Dauphin Island and Mobile Point. The troops that were saved from those vessels were landed on Mobile Point together with the rest of the army where they remained a few days until on the 15th they were landed with their artillery a mile below Mobile.

Polacre

As the Spanish approached the entrance to Mobile Bay they saw a British ship of 16 guns, aground on the west side of the channel opposite Mobile Point. Despite a storm from the southwest and heavy seas[105] the 20 gun frigate *El Volante* led

---

[105] *Alabama and the Borderlands*, Coker and Coker; *The Siege of Mobile, 1780, in Maps*, page 172. Hamilton in *Colonial Mobile* suggests there was a hurricane. Coker does not give us the name of the British ship.

the way into the Bay and promptly went aground on the west side of the channel just north of the present location of Sand Island Light. When the British crew recognized the Spaniards, they abandoned ship and took to their pulling boats. The *Galvez,* Captain Rousseau, and four of the other ships also ran aground on the banks or sandbars as they attempted to enter. All efforts failed to free the *Volante* and two other ships but by 1 AM on the 11th the Spaniards had freed the *Galvez,* which had suffered damage and was taking 9 inches of water an hour.

Captain Pickles accompanied the Spanish fleet with Galvez to Mobile and apparently managed to enter the Bay without mishap. The ships armament had been upgraded by Pollock and now mounted four 6 pounders and 12 swivel guns.[106] First Officer Pierre Rousseau who was with Pickles when he captured the *West Florida* was no longer with him. Rousseau had entered the Spanish service under Galvez and was Captain of the Brigantine [107] *Galvez* which we shall see was also known as the *Galvestown.* According to an affidavit signed by Rousseau at

Fort Charlotte reconstructed

---

[106] *George Gauld, Surveyor and Cartographer of the Gulf Coast* by Robert R. Rea, University of Florida Press, page 21.

[107] A brig is a two masted square-rigged ship with an additional gaff sail on the mainmast. A Brigantine is almost exactly the same but without the gaff sail, and the mainmast is fore and aft rigged.

New Orleans on November 15, 1803 in which he was petitioning for a pension he stated that he had a part in: "the conquest of Movila (Mobile), as commander of the above mentioned *Galvezton*." [108]

Since much has been written on the siege of Mobile I shall only summarize the events.[109]

The siege of Mobile was to be a siege of the French Fort Condé, built by the French in 1717. The British renamed it Fort Charlotte and added to its brick and mortar walls and had mounted between its four bastions over 30 guns. The defenders were 300 men from the fourth Battalion of the 60th regiment, the Royal artillery, engineers, Pennsylvania and Maryland Tories, local volunteers and a number of Negroes. It was commanded by Capt. Elias Durnford, a British Army engineer and former lieutenant governor of West Florida. The garrison made their stand in the brick Fort

Captain Elias Durnford commander British forces at Mobile

---

[108] *Rousseau: The Last Days of Spanish New Orleans* by Raymond J. Martinez with forward by Jack D. L. Holmes, page 116.
[109] See among other references *Colonial Mobile* by Peter Joseph Hamilton, pages 310 – 315 and *Honor And Fidelity* by Jack D. L. Holmes pages 31-33.

awaiting reinforcements from Pensacola.

The groundings and sinkings opposite Mobile Point cost the Spanish ships, men and material and left them disorganized. Fortunately, five ships of the expected Havana fleet arrived with some 600 troops and supplies and with the welcome information that additional reinforcements were to follow. With that information in hand Galvez decided to proceed with the attack. Fortunately for the Spanish the British at Mobile were even more disorganized. The British lost their best opportunity for attacking before Galvez was able to regroup. After a few days at Mobile Point Galvez landed troops and artillery at Choctaw Point and Dog River below Mobile.

During the confusion as the citizens herded into Fort Charlotte Galvez erected six batteries north and west of the Fort and began a brisk bombardment. The British burned the intervening houses to clear their field of fire. Galvez's forces outnumbered and out gunned at the point of attack the British during the siege. No counter attack was forthcoming from Pensacola. The total British forces at Mobile were about 300 men. The force available to Galvez was almost 2000. The Spanish batteries soon affected a breach in the walls of the fort which capitulated on March 14, 1780. Under the surrender terms the garrison agreed they would not fight against Spain for 18 months. The agreement did not preclude fighting the revolting colonies. Most of the garrison was transported to New York where they were available for service against the rebels. The armed colonist to assisted in the defense were treated as prisoners of war. The Spanish troops entered Fort Charlotte in August 1780.

Diorama of the siege of Fort Charlotte-1780

A relief force from Pensacola under General Campbell of 522 men was on the east side of the Mobile River Delta at Tensa building rafts. When Fort Charlotte surrendered they marched back through the wilderness to Pensacola to await the Spanish fleet and siege cannons the following year. For them there was to be no relief fleet or column.

General Campbell did make one further attempt to retake or at least harass the Spanish in Mobile. The Spanish had built an outpost on the east side of the bay at French Village in the present-day Montrose area where they secured their drinking water. On 3 January 1781 Captain Von Hanxleden with 100 infantrymen of the 60th Regiment, 11 militia cavalry, 300 Indians, and 60 Waldeckers set out from Pensacola to drive the Spaniards out of their fort or entrenchments. The force arrived in front of the Spanish on January 7 and made several bloody attempts to storm the Spanish works. The Spanish held and the British again marched back to Pensacola.[110]

Negotiating the surrender of the fort. Alabama Department of Archives and History.

---

[110] Hamilton, *Colonial Mobile*, page 315-317; *German Mercenaries in Pensacola during the American Revolution, 1779 – 1781*, translated by Louis Krupp 1938, Pensacola Historical Society, November, 1977.

There was mention above that the Navy considered the gulf coast to be a hardship posting. General Campbell considered it likewise. In a letter to Sir Henry Clinton dated May 18, 1780 Campbell stated that it grieved him that he had not sufficient strength to act offensively and pleaded for reinforcements. "Otherwise permit me to solicit your Excellency for permission to join the Army, rather than remain here, with such troops as compose my pitiful command, without the least chance of serving with credit to myself or with honor an advantage to my royal master, – pestered with innumerable difficulties, and a multiplicity of perplexing business – you may therefore conceive my feelings in my present situation, which I humbly submit to your serious consideration." Campbell was not allowed to resign nor did he receive any reinforcements.[111]

Captain Pickles and the *West Florida* were credited with playing an important part in the Spanish victory at Mobile. Oliver Pollock was present as an aide-de-camp to Galvez probably with his nine "brother Americans" that accompanied him on the Natchez campaign. At the outbreak of the war between Spain and Britain there were a number of individuals from the United States, West and East Florida and Nova Scotia in New Orleans. They were all required to take an oath of fidelity to the King of Spain during their residence in his dominions, or immediately depart. It appears the oath was

---

[111] *Report on American Manuscripts in the Royal Institution of Great Britain*, volume 2, page 124, 1906.

taken by eighty-three individuals.[112] Since the "American English" at New Orleans had been forced to take an oath to the King of Spain at the outbreak of the war it is probable that there were a number of participants who resided in New Orleans but considered themselves as United States citizens.

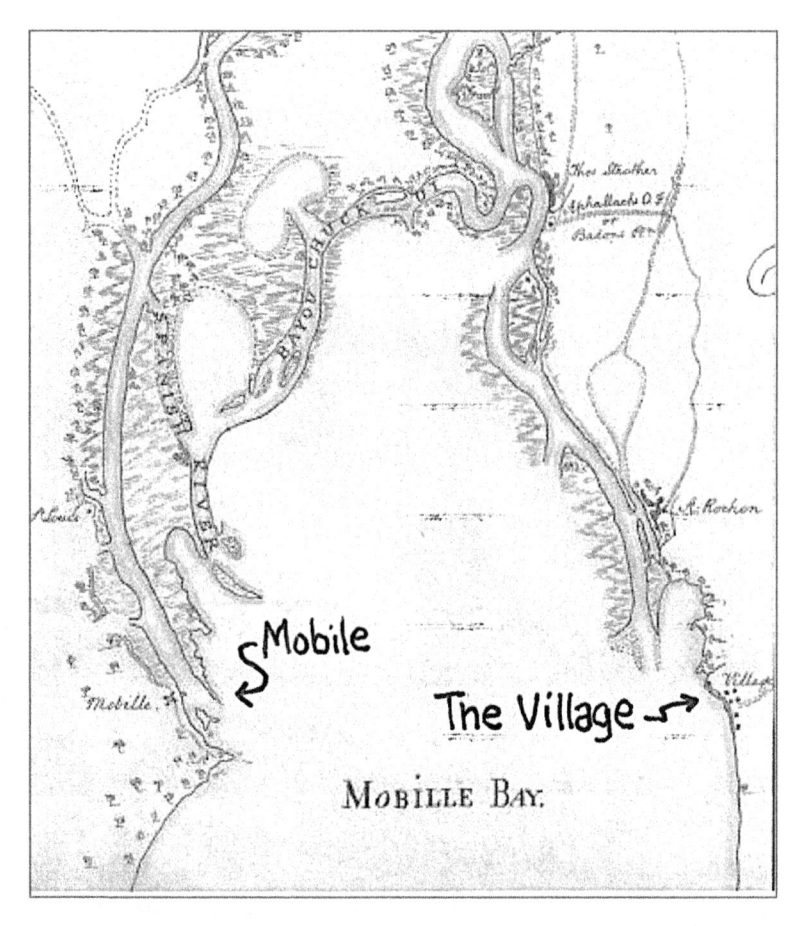

Map of Mobile area by British Surveyor David Taitt - 1772

---

[112] *The History of Louisiana* by Francois-Xavier Martin, New Orleans, 1882.

Six pounder guns were not siege weapons and would not do much damage to the walls of a brick fort. The *West Florida*, armed with such guns, was stationed at one time during the siege near the site of the present-day battleship Alabama.

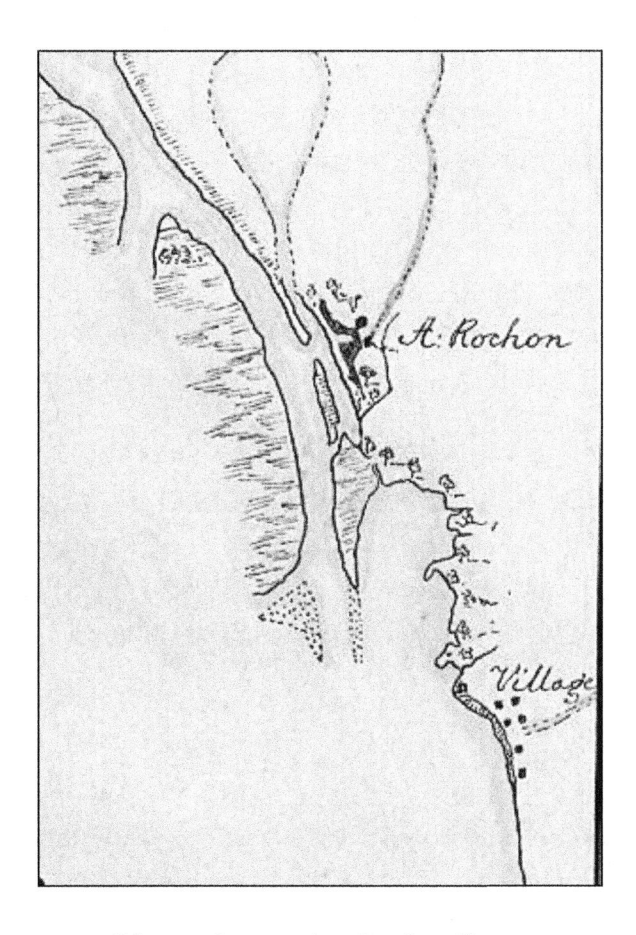

Detail from Taitt Map showing the Village

Captain Elias Durnford British commander at Mobile reported to his commander General Campbell at Pensacola: "the vessels I can see from this place [Fort Charlotte] are in the mouth of the East Pass, about 2 miles distance from the Fort. And the *Galvez* Brig is one and Pickler's *Florida* the other. Near to the Dog River are five ships or pollacas, and I am informed that three or four are in Dog River, besides the Row Galley."[113] Ships that came within range of the larger guns of the Fort could be in trouble. At one point during the siege a Spanish row galley was on station opposite Choctaw Point where her cable was cut and the British were certain that three 9 pounder shot struck her sending her off to Dog River to repair the damage.[114]

Captain Joseph Calvert, an American privateersman who visited Mobile during the siege credited Pickles of having been "of greatest service" to Galvez. Pollock conveyed the same sentiments to Congress and Congress Recognized Pickles for his service. The *West Florida* captured a small British sloop in Mobile Bay which John Henderson, Pollock's clerk, sold as a prize at Mobile.[115]

---

[113] Hamilton, *Colonial Mobile*, page 315. See also *The Founding of Mobile* by Caldwell Delaney, 1994 and *From Fort to Port* by Elizabeth Barrett Gould, 1988.

[114] *A History of Louisiana, volume 2*, printed 1904, pages 72 – 73, by Alcee Fortier.

[115] Pollock reported to the commercial committee of Congress that Captain Calvert had agreed to touch at Mobile or Pensacola "in order that you may have news as soon as possible for your government". *Alabama and the Borderlands*, page 217, note 24.

Rendering of the reconstructed Fort Conde/Charlotte

Sold out of Service

With his work done at Mobile Captain Pickles was released by Galvez and Pollock and proceeded with the *West Florida* to Havana. The *West Florida* arrived in Philadelphia about June 1, 1780 with news of the capture Of Mobile.[116] Upon her arrival she was surveyed and based on such the Board of Admiralty[117] concluded she was not fit as a cruiser. That verdict is not surprising since a year and a half before surveyors at Pensacola had concluded: "she will not run longer than six months except she gets a new bottom". After she was captured by Pickles she was outfitted with heavier guns and Pollock may have undertaken some repairs but there is no indication nor does there appear to have been enough time to have given her a new bottom. In any event the journals of Congress show that on June 7, 1780 Congress concurred and ordered "that the Board of Admiralty cause sale to be made at public auction of the sloop *West Florida*, and pay the proceeds into the treasury of the United States, to be applied to the use of the navy; and that the crew of the said sloop be turned over to the ships of war now fitting out in this harbor."[118] Thus ended the career of

---

[116] *The Navy of the American Revolution* by Charles Oscar Paullin, 1906, page 311.

[117] On October 28, 1779 Congress replaced the cumbersome Marine Committee with a five person Board of Admiralty to handle naval and maritime affairs, Chapelle, *The American Sailing Navy*, page 87.

[118] Philadelphia.

the U.S.S. *West Florida,* but not the naval career of her Captain, William Pickles.

The final chapter in the story of the Revolutionary Navy on the Mississippi and upper Gulf coast involved the settling up of accounts between Captain Pickles, his crew and Congress.

Congress received a report from the board of Admiralty dated December 5, 1780 which, after reciting the capture and career of the sloop *West Florida* noted that Captain Pickles as agent for his crew had appointed Mr. Joseph Pennell (pay master for the Navy Board) as his attorney for the purpose of paying such of the crew as may apply their respective shares of the $2700 (being the value of the vessel upon capture and thus the value of prize money to be distributed). Mr. Pennell advised the board that there was a further sum of $359 belonging to the crew, for which they have claim upon the public, making the whole amount of the prize money $3059, of which Captain Pickles had paid the officers and men, then under his command, about 1470 hard dollars. Captain Pickles was very anxious to pay his people their prize money before he went away, but "had it not in his power". Captain Pickles had been obliged to borrow money for his expenses here which was then unpaid. The board then submitted a resolution to the board of treasury that a warrant for such sums were to be issued in favor of Captain Pickles attorney "for the purpose of paying the several claimants, their proportion of the value of the sloop of war *West*

Florida, and that the disposition of the said money be under the direction of the board of Admiralty."[119]

Captain Pickles and the Packet *Mercury*

A packet service, to be maintained with three vessels between America and France, was established by the Continental Congress in 1780. The service was under the control of the Board of Admiralty that succeeded the Marine Committee.

Congress had authorized the building of three packets in 1776 and three more were ordered in 1780. One of the vessels authorized in 1776 was the packet *Mercury* built by Josiah Humphreys in Philadelphia. The 1780 authorization vessels were built from a design by John Peck at Plymouth, Massachusetts and one of those was also named the *Mercury*. Packets were to be swift vessels and while not intended as warships their service in maintaining communications with Europe was high on Congress' priorities.

In 1780 Henry Laurens was sent on a diplomatic mission as United States Minister to the Dutch Republic. His transportation was to be the new Humphreys' built Continental Packet *Mercury* under the command of Captain William Pickles.

---

[119] *Journals of the Continental Congress 1774 – 1789*, volume 18, 1780, Washington, Government Printing Office, 1910.

Laurens was first named a delegate to the Continental Congress on January 10, 1977. He served in the Congress until 1780. He was the president of the Continental Congress from November 1, 1777 to December 9, 1778.

Pickles orders from the board of Admiralty dated August 11, 1780 was as follows: "Sir – The Board of Admiralty having appointed you to command the Continental packet *Mercury*, you are hereby ordered to proceed with all possible dispatch north about for Amsterdam in the United Provinces of the Netherlands, where, when you arrive, you are to receive on board the *Mercury* all such articles as the Hon. Henry Laurens shall by himself or his agents order to be put on board, when the *Mercury* is completed laden, you are to proceed on your return with the vessel for any safe port on the coast of North America giving Philadelphia, Chesapeake Bay, or Egg Harbor the preference and give this board immediate notice of your arrival. –

Henry Laurens

"You will make all dispatch in your power while in Amsterdam so that you may arrive on this coast before the winter sets in.

"You are at liberty to take passengers on your homeward bound voyage, but no articles but such as each of them may bring in a trunk of a midling size, and no private property for any person, but such as Mr. Laurens may direct you to receive, and be governed by his orders during your voyage. Mr. Laurens will advance you for your crew the monies we have agreed shall be paid them at Amsterdam agreeable to your shipping bill. The board desire that you will make Mr. Laurens passage as comfortable as possible and that you will at all times exercise economy and dispatch. –

"Wishing you a prosperous voyage I am Sir – your humble servant – by order– John Brown Sec."

In response to inquiries from George Washington the Board on August 14 advised him that: "the Continental Armed Ship *Saratoga* John Young Commander went down the River yesterday in order to convey the Hon. Henry Laurens Esq in the *Mercury* Packet a few leagues to sea, then to return within the Capes."[120]

Captain Pickles *Mercury* departed Port Penn August 13, 1780. Pickles was governed by the orders of Laurens on the voyage. On August 19 the *Mercury* sailed to sea under convoy of the Continental ship-rigged sloop the *Saratoga* of about 18 guns. The orders for the *Saratoga* had changed and she was to

---

[120] *Out-Letters of the Continental Marine Committee and Board of Admiralty, August, 1776 – September, 1780*, edited by Charles Oscar Paullin of the Carnegie Institute of Washington, volume 2, pages 234 – 243.

accompany the *Mercury* to the Grand Banks and then proceed on her first cruise.[121]

On August 23 Laurens ordered four 4-pounder cannons out of the packet to the *Saratoga*. The winds being unfavorable for going northward Laurens ordered Pickles to shape for any port from L'Orient to Cadiz. The *Mercury* was a faster sailor than the *Saratoga* so she had to shorten sail each night slowing her progress. Laurens decided to proceed without the escort of the *Saratoga*.

On September 3, 1780 the Mercury was captured off the banks of Newfoundland by the 28 gun British frigate *Vestal*. Laurens described the capture as follows: at first light ("first dawn of day") a sail was sighted to leeward. Pickles put *Mercury* close to the wind. Laurens was of the opinion that if left before the wind the frigate could not have come up to her but Pickles decided to put her before the wind, which Laurens considered to be her worst point of sailing, especially as she was badly ballasted with sand. About 9:00 AM the frigate began to fire her bow guns. At 11 o'clock her shot went over the *Mercury* and two between her masts. Pickles then hauled down the flag. Laurens threw his papers overboard in a bag with 20 or 25 pounds of shot. The bag did not sink and was hauled up by the *Vestal*. Found in his papers was the draft of a possible U. S. - Dutch treaty prepared by William Lee. This find prompted Britain to declare war on the Netherlands, which became known

---

[121] Howard I. Chapelle, *The History of the American Sailing Navy*, page 86. The *Saratoga* was lost at sea on this first cruise.

as the fourth Anglo – Dutch war. Laurens papers were much talked about in Europe.[122]

Laurens in his papers said that the *Mercury* was a Brigantine. According to Chapelle[123] her captors, H.B.M. Ships *Fairy* and *Vestial,* stated that the *Mercury* was a new ketch rigged vessel 72'5" long on the main deck, 20'5" beam and 8'8" depth of hold.

Pickles and Laurens were imprisoned in London. After his release Pickles returned to Philadelphia where he died on September 9, 1783 from injuries resulting from an assault by a gang of Italian sailors. The prosecution of his murderers was complicated by legal questions i.e. whether statutes previously enacted by the British Parliament were still in force in the now independent state of Pennsylvania. Two of the sailors were sentenced on October 8, 1783 to hang 10 days later.[124]

---

[122] *Papers of Henry Laurens*, volume 15.
[123] Howard I. Chapelle, *The history of the American sailing Navy*, pages 86 – 87.
[124] *Papers of Henry Laurens,* volume 15; *Report of Cases Ruled That Adjust in the Courts of Pennsylvania, before and since the Revolution*, Volume 1; *Pennsylvania Colonial Records*, Volume 13.

The Spanish Replica of the Continental Sloop *Galveztown/West Florida*

A shipyard in Malaga, Spain, in association with the Lighthouse Museum of St. Augustine, Florida, started building in 2008 a replica of the *West Florida* and when completed intends to sail her to St. Augustine and then to the Gulf Coast. Actually, they are building a replica of the brigantine *Galveston*, or given the absence of builders plans a period brigantine approximating as close as their research allows the *Galveztown* upon which general Galvez won fame and honor in 1781 by running her past the guns of the forts at the entrance to Pensacola Bay while the Spanish Havana fleet, having concluded that such was too risky, lay anchored outside.

The shipyard, Astilleros Nereo and its collaborator the Lighthouse Archaeological Maritime Program (LAMP), the research arm of the St. Augustine lighthouse and Museum has for a number of years taken the position that the Brigantine *Galveztown* was the renamed sloop *West Florida.* This position as well as their belief that the *Galveztown* was named after Galveston, Texas is understandable since some well-known historians have reached those same conclusions, at least as to the communality of the ships. I disagree with them on both issues and over several years have corresponded with both Spain and St. Augustine from time to time, but their stated positions on both questions remains unchanged.

It would please me very much to see a replica of the sloop *West Florida* sail up Mobile Bay with all of her flags, including a huge Galvez personal Yo Solo flag, even if the builders call it the Brigantine *Galveztown/West Florida*. But history is history.

I have related above the history of the sloop *West Florida* from the time she was bought in by the British Navy until she was sold out of service by the Continental Navy. Let me now relate to you some background as to how my nearly 40 year research project on Mobile's connection to the Continental Navy in 1780 began, where it has led me, how the history of those vessels are connected and how such shows they are not one and the same.

But first let me address the periphery issue as to whether the *Galveztown* was named for Galveston, Texas or Galveztown, Louisiana. In the discussion and press releases on the building of the replica of the Brigantine *Galveston* it is stated that the vessel *Galveztown* was named after the city of Galveston, Texas. Hurricane Ike swamped that city on September 13, 2008 and killed by salt water incursion an estimated 40,000 trees.[125] Damaged wood from hurricane Ike has been shipped from Galveston to Malaga, Spain to be used in the replica.

French explorer LaSalle named Galveston Island, which he discovered, in honor of the French king, "San Luis," a name it

---

[125] *The Keepers Blog*, June 8, 2010, an Internet publication of the St. Augustine Lighthouse and Museum.

retained for many years. As late as 1821 the island was still called San Luis by a New Orleans newspaper. The Spaniards, however when they acquired Texas with Mexico, called the island Culebra or Snake Island, and a small sister island then in existence to the east they called Little Culebra Island. The name of San Luis Island after 1825 was applied to the island west of Galveston Island. The name of Galveston Island was given after pirate Lafitte called his settlement there Galvez Town in 1819. The small Culebra Island Lafitte renamed Campeche.

Galveston was not named directly to honor Bernardo de Galvez, but rather a quartel or garrison fort on the Trinity River, near Liberty was named for the famous Governor. In 1835 a hurricane filled up the pass through which Lafitte sailed his vessels and little Campeche ceased to exist and the two islands became the present island of Galveston.[126] Others have been more specific: "during his charting of the Gulf coast in 1785, the Spanish explorer José de Evia named the island Galvez – Town after Bernardo de Galvez y Madrid, Count of Galvez."[127]

Whether Galveston, Texas received its name in 1785 or 1835 is an interesting question but not relevant to the question as to whether the brigantine *Galveston* of Pensacola Bay fame was the renamed sloop *West Florida*. The Brigantine/Brig *Galveztown* was at Mobile in 1780 and Pensacola in 1781. She

---

[126] *Galveston* by Dr. J. O. Dyer, Centenary edition part one, page 2.
[127] *Galveston a History* by David G. McComb, University of Texas Press.

then could not have been named for the Texas island which did not receive its name until several years later.

There is a Louisiana State Historical Marker located in Galvez, Louisiana near Port Vincent, Ascension Parish that reads: "Galveztown – old Spanish town at junction of Amite River and Bayou Manchac. Settled by Anglo – Americans, 1776 – 78, seeking Spanish refuge from American Revolution, and by Canary Islanders (Islenos). Named for Spanish Governor Bernardo de Galvez. The town was abandoned by 1810." The grateful Americans allowed to settle in Spanish territory to escape the hostilities in the Colonies asked Galvez for and received permission to name their settlement "Galveztown". Galvez realized the strategic importance of the town and began bringing in Spanish settlers from the Canary Islands. He also placed troops in and built fortifications around the town. [128]

I have found no period documentation stating that the ship was named for the Louisiana town. The fact that the Texas town did not receive its name until some years later indicates that it must necessarily have been named for Galvez – Town, Louisiana. No less an authority on the Spanish period in New Orleans and West Florida than Jack D. H. Holmes has taken that position. In his foreword to the book Rousseau: The Last Days of Spanish New Orleans at page II he states: "The captured British vessel *West Florida* was renamed the *Galvez - Town*, in honor of the new settlement of Canary Island immigrants located on the

---

[128] *De Bow's Review of the Southern and Western States*, Volume 11 – new series, volume 14, New Orleans 1851, page 254; *BayouManchac.org*.

Amite River, just below its confluence with Bayou Manchac." There are no footnotes in the forward which was dated March 1974 but there is an impressive list of sources at page VIII.

Was the *Galveztown* the *West Florida?*

Researching

In the early 1970s I drafted a Bicentennial celebration plan for the City of Mobile for a tourism committee of the Mobile Chamber of Commerce. The plan was never adopted notwithstanding its brilliance, as perceived by me. Consequently at the time I was focused on and was on the lookout for Continental connections to Mobile. In 1975 I came across a reference in an issue of *The Naval Institute Proceedings* published by the Naval Historical Section in Washington that mentioned that a Continental naval vessel the *West Florida* was part of Galvez's fleet during the siege of Mobile in 1780. I was an avid reader of local history and was building a library on all things local be it naval, Indians, Civil War, railroads, aircraft and ships and steamboats in general. To me the fact that there was a Continental naval presence in Mobile as part of Mobile's Revolutionary War battle was important, albeit the battle was between the British and Spanish, so I began the research which more than forty years later resulted in this book the first draft of which was prepared as a paper in 1976. It took those intervening years to complete because after the Bicentennial it was no longer at the top of my priority list, I had a number of other projects underway and the pertinent documents were in Spain and London and the National Archives in Washington.

Early in 1976 Dr. William J. Morgan of the Naval History Division in Washington and editor of the *Naval Institute Proceedings* was scheduled to present a paper on some naval history subject to a military history conference at the University of Alabama in Tuscaloosa. I knew Dr. Morgan was familiar with Civil War Mobile Bay as he had worked with the Smithsonian on an exploratory excavation of the monitor *Tecumseh* which was sunk during the Battle of Mobile Bay off Fort Morgan. I loaded my friend David Smithweck into my car and we drove from Mobile to Tuscaloosa to hear his talk but primarily to meet him. In a letter to Dr. Morgan dated February 2, 1976 I stated: "At the Military History Conference at the University of Alabama you kindly offered to attempt to answer specific naval history questions." I then proceeded with several paragraphs of such questions (to which he in due course graciously responded) and ended the letter with this postscript: "The information you gave me in Tuscaloosa concerning the *West Florida* (Captain William Pickles) was most helpful. I have found some information on the *West Florida* in the *Navy of the American Revolution* by Charles Oscar Paullin and I have ordered a copy of the biography of Oliver Pollock which should give me the full story concerning the *West Florida's* participation in the capture of Mobile."

I found those books to be helpful but they could not provide me with the details of the battle or the relative strength of the vessels. I had already completed a search of the local histories and found in Peter Joseph Hamilton's book, *Colonial Mobile*, the local British commanders report where he stated that the vessels he could see included "Pickler's *Florida*" with no mention that the "*Florida*" (*West Florida*) was a Continental vessel. Local historians Caldwell Delaney and Jay Higginbotham both told me that they were unaware that the vessel referred to in Hamilton's book was a Continental vessel.

I was not necessarily on my own since I continued to call on the Naval History Division. Dr. Morgan retired in the early 80s and then his successor Dr. William Dudley and researcher Dr. Crawford provided me with British and Spanish references which eventually led me to receiving first-hand participant reports. The Naval History Division was publishing from time to time volumes of their multiple volume *Naval Documents of the American Revolution*. By 1985 Volume 9 was published but that covered only through 1777. With the Naval researchers assurances that all the relevant American documents would be published in due course I was content to wait for those and used the several weeks that I spent in the National Archives over a period of years working on other projects. After I retired from my law practice the volumes that covered 1780 and 81 were in the stacks of University of South Alabama Library and with a search of those I thought I had completed my search for documents and would be able to put my collected material on paper, but first I had other research projects including a book on Fort Powell to be completed. [129]

Frames for the Galveztown/West Florida being erected at Malaga, Spain

I find the Internet to be a marvelous research tool as long such sites are thoroughly vetted by checking sources. *Google Books* is an excellent resource of fully downloadable antique out-of-print books together with snippets of more recent books that still might be available in hard copy. Thinking that I had completed my research in 2008 I did what I thought was one final internet search for "the continental sloop *West Florida*". I was somewhat surprised when my Google search turned up numerous articles relating to the replica of the *Galveztown* by the St. Augustine Lighthouse group, by a

---

[129] Now published as *Fort Powell and the Civil War Western Approaches to Mobile Bay 1861-1865*, Heritage Books, 2012.

shipyard in Spain and by St. Augustine and Galveston, Texas newspapers.

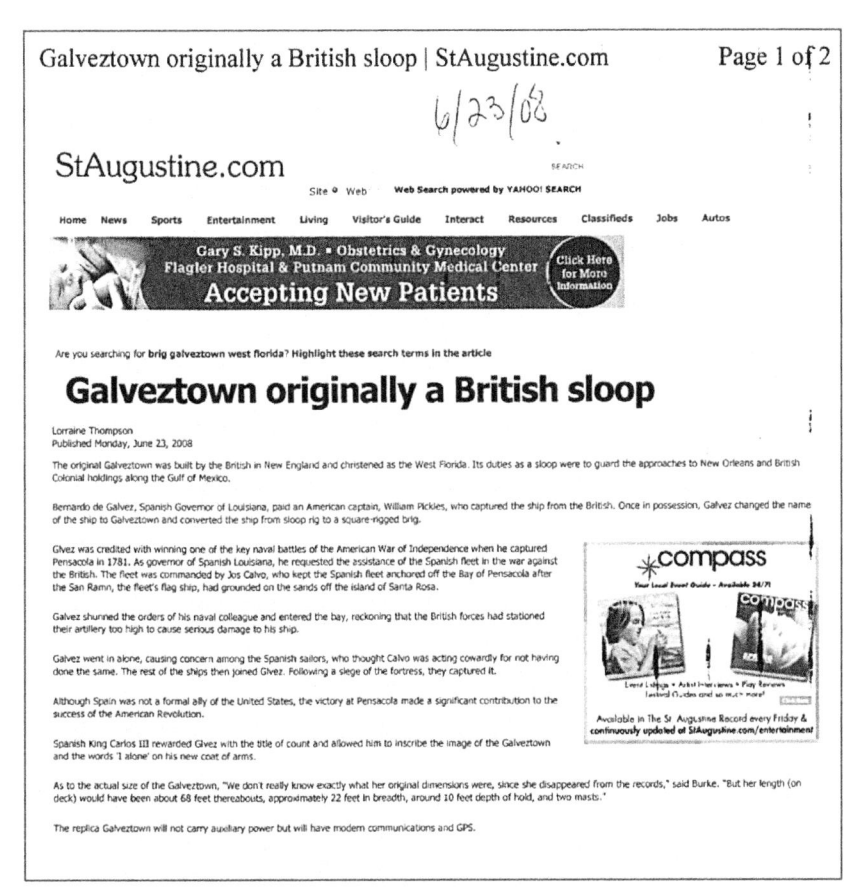

Internet publication of StAugustine.com re the *West Florida*

The common theme through those articles was that the Brigantine *Galveston*, of Pensacola fame, was the renamed Captain Pickles *West Florida*. StAugustine.com an Internet publication dated June 23, 2008 said: "The Original *Galveztown* was built by the British in New England and christened as the *West Florida*. It's duties as a sloop was to guard the approaches to New Orleans and British colonial holdings along the Gulf of Mexico. Bernardo de Galvez, Spanish Governor of Louisiana, paid an American captain, William Pickles, who captured the ship from the British. Once in possession, Galvez changed the name of the ship to *Galveston* and converted the ship from sloop rig to square – rigged brig." [130]

It is totally understandable that even a good researcher relying on published sources would conclude that the *Galveztown* and the *West Florida* was the same vessel. In the foreword to the book *Rousseau: The Last Days of Spanish New Orleans* at page II, Jack D. H. Holmes states: "The captured British vessel *West Florida* was renamed the *Galvez-Town*, in honor of the new settlement of Canary Island immigrants located on the Amite River, just below its confluence with Bayou Manchac." He also writes in his book *Honor and Fidelity* at page 33 that Rousseau's *Galveztown* at Pensacola was the renamed *West Florida*.

---

[130] Among Other Articles: *LAMPS* by the St. Augustine lighthouse and Museum, April 17, 2008; Jacksonville.com dated July 27, 2011; *Houston Chronicle* dated June 8, 2010; *Wikipedia* as last modified January 9, 2013.

Detail of a period drawing of the Brigantine Galveztown in Pensacola Bay

By the time I found the Internet references to the construction of the replica in Malaga Spain and read that the researchers involved in that project had concluded that their under construction replica was formally the British sloop *West Florida* I had already reached the conclusion that it was not. I then send e-mails to St. Augustine and to the Museum Shipyard Astilleros Nereo in Malaga noting their positions that the vessels were the same and asking them to please send to me a citation to or a copy of the document showing that the vessels were one and the same. In response I was referred to page 116 of the book *Rousseau: The Last Days of Spanish New Orleans* a book written as a family history by a descendant of Rousseau. I ordered the book and upon receipt found at page 116 a petition for a pension signed by Rousseau, at New Orleans, November 15, 1803. Numbered paragraph 3 on page 116 states: "That he had a part in the conquest of Mobile, as commander of the above-mentioned *Galveston*." The statement by Rousseau is directly contradictory to Jack Holmes statement in the forward and is further contradicted on page 15 of the book where the author states, citing Paullin, that after aiding in the capture of Mobile and taking a small prize the *West Florida* proceeded to Philadelphia, where she arrived about 1 June, 1780. The author then concluded: "certainly, she did not then take part in the 'reduction' of Pensacola for that did not occur until in March of 1781."

With that information in hand I sent e-mails to St. Augustine and Spain pointing out why I thought the book *Rousseau* did not answer the question and sent along a timeline showing each documented event that I had been able to find in the life of the sloop *West Florida*.

While still posting in newsletters etc. on the Internet that the vessels are one and the same the reasons for such position has shifted and now is apparently based upon their understanding that the Spanish purchased the vessel at auction in 1780 in Philadelphia, renamed her the *Galveztown*, brought her to New Orleans then to Havana and then to the siege of Pensacola in 1781.[131] If so and if the replica is completed and

---

[131] *Houston Chronicle*, January 29, 2012. This article is captioned "brig *Galveston* delayed in interest of accuracy." The article relates that construction of the replica has been halted because an

sails into Mobile harbor we locals would be able to point to her and say that is a replica of the renamed *West Florida* which was Mobile's naval link to the American Revolution.

I requested from St. Augustine and Malaga a copy of such documentation on several occasions over the last several years and I still hope to receive such.

I shall now review the reasons why I do not think the *Galveztown* was the renamed sloop *West Florida*.

First, let us do a comparison of the size of the vessels. The *West Florida* was a small vessel. When purchased by the British Navy she was described as being 60 tons and drawing 6 feet of water at the stern. The British armed her with two 6-pounders and two 4-pounders. Swivels are not generally included in the listing of the main armament of vessels. The Americans upgraded her armament to four 6-pounders. In the log of *HMS Mentor 1780 – 1781* The editor noted that the *Hound*, *Stork* and *Sylph*, ships then at Pensacola, were mere 14 gun sloops and that the *West Florida* was even smaller.

---

architect found more details about the original design of the ship. The keel design for a 68 foot on deck length had already been placed when they learned that the original on deck length was 56 feet, a full 12 feet shorter than originally thought. Naval architect Francisco Fernandez said he discovered the original dimensions by piecing together information from documents in the United States, Spain and Great Britain. Quoting Sam Turner of the Lighthouse Museum: "the end result is going to be a very accurate replica of an 18th-century brig."

I have found no dimensions on the *Galveztown*. In the proceedings of the Gulf Coast history and humanities conference published 1982 entitled *Anglo – Spanish Confrontation on the Gulf Coast During the American Revolution* edited by William S. Coker and Robert R. Rea in the Eric Beerman paper *Jose Solano and the Spanish Navy at the Siege of Pensacola*, at page 132, relying apparently the *Diary of Pensacola* by Francisco De Miranda, Beerman states that the *Galvestown* was armed with twenty 4-pounders. Beerman also says at page 132 that General Galvez took the *Galvestown* up the middle River at Pensacola in an unsuccessful attempt to find the British frigate *Mentor*. The *Mentor* was a 220 to 250 ton vessel with a draught of 14 feet. She was armed with eighteen 12-pounders on the gun deck and six 4-pound guns on the quarter deck. It is not likely that Galvez in a four gun ex *West Florida* would have sought out a confrontation with a 24 gun ship with a main battery of 12-pounders.

Contemporary drawings of the siege of Pensacola show the *Galveztown* pierced for five guns on each side. The Yo Solo *Galveztown* added to the coat of arms of General Galvez also depicts a vessel pierced for five guns on each side. The artist rendering those vessels may or may not have been on the scene and may have been simply depicting a generic small period brigantine.

One indication as to the size of the *Galveztown* was found in the letter to Congress to Oliver Pollock dated April 26, 1780, quoted previously, noting that Pollock was with General

Galvez coat of arms with Galvez and the *Galveztown* in the right center. The King granted to him the banner of Yo Solo or I Alone.

Galvez when he sailed from New Orleans early in February 1780 with his fleet bound for Mobile. The fleet was described as consisting of a 20 gun ship the *Ventura* which was lost off Mobile point and "two 14 or 16 gun brigs" and other vessels apparently with fewer guns. We know that the brig *Galvez/Galveztown* was with the fleet which would mean that she was probably one of the 14 or 16 gun brigs. She well could have been upgraded to 20 4-pounders, as Beerman states above, within the next year prior to the siege of Pensacola.

I have discussed above the book *Rousseau* by Raymond J. Martinez wherein Jack D.L. Holmes in his foreword stated that the *Galveztown* was the renamed *West Florida*. Martinez at page 116 quotes from a petition for a pension signed by Rousseau which states that Rousseau participated in the conquest of Mobile as commander of the *Galveztown*. Martinez does not, however, quote the entire document and omits the following pertinent portion: "Gen. Don Bernardo de Galvez appointed him (referring to Rousseau) to the command of the brigantine named '*Galveztown*' at the beginning of the war declared against Great Britain." [132]

The fact that Rousseau was given the *West Florida* as prize captain immediately after she was captured could be a part of the confusion. But the prize captain's job usually is simply to get the captured vessel to a safe port which was only a

---

[132] *The Spanish Regime in Missouri* by Lewis Houk, volume 2 printed 1909, page 324.

few miles away at Fort St. John or a day's sail to New Orleans. Most likely he took the captured *West Florida* to Fort St. John from whence he traveled through the bayou to New Orleans or he took the *Caindre* to New Orleans where he was commissioned into the Louisiana militia and given command by Governor Galvez of the Spanish flag privately owned vessel the *Galveztown*. He certainly did not remain as prize captain more than a few days because Captain Pickles was cruising with her during the following month on Lake Pontchartrain.

Detail from the Bernardo De Galvez coat of arms

I find no record of any connection between Rousseau and the sloop *West Florida* after the battle.

Galvez reported in his journal that there was with his fleet when it left New Orleans the "privateer brig *El Galvez*".[133] Prior to arriving in Mobile Galvez boarded his ship the "*Galvez*". At Pensacola a year later there are references to the *Galveztown* as a private vessel controlled by Galvez. The records show that it was the *Galvez* that was blown aground at the entrance to Mobile Bay. The British commander at Mobile reported that he had both the *Galvez* and "Pickler's *Florida*" in sight at the same time.

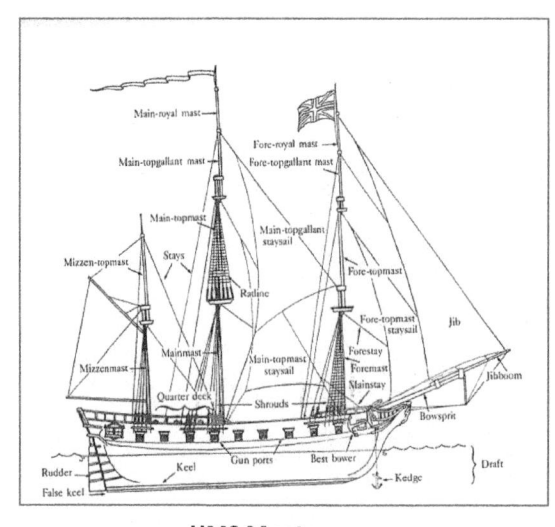

HMS Mentor

Later at Pensacola it was clear from the log entries of the British frigate *Mentor* that the *Galvez/Galveztown* was known to them as it was mentioned several times as the *Galvez*. In Major Robert Farmar's *Journal of the siege of Pensacola* he on three occasions refers to the *Galveztown*. When that vessel first entered the harbor with Galvez aboard Farmar referred to it as "*Galvez's brig*". On two other occasions he referred to it as simply "*the Galvez brig*".

---

[133] *Journal of Don Bernardo De Galvez* translated from the Madrid Gazette, dated Mobile, March 20, 1780.

Domingo Flectas served as a medic-in-chief with Galvez at the capture of Fort Bute at Manchac and Baton Rouge in 1779. On the expedition to Mobile he was serving on the *Santa Catalina*, alias La *Ventura* which was lost off Mobile Point in 1780. Following the loss of the *Ventura* he served as surgeon major on the Spanish brigantine *Galveztown* from June 14, 1780.[134] The evidence seems overwhelming that the *Galveztown* was at Mobile under Rousseau.

After the completion of the siege of Mobile Pickles proceeded with the *West Florida* to Havana and then to Philadelphia arriving there about June 1, 1780. Later that same month the *West Florida* was sold out of Continental service.

The latest newspaper articles and postings concerning the replica *Galveztown* state that she was bought by General Galvez and renamed the *Galveztown* and was under the command of Rousseau at the siege of Pensacola. The records show that the *Galvestown*, lately from New Orleans, sailed from Havana on March 2 and joined the fleet off Pensacola March 5, 1781. Certainly there was time between the sale of the *West Florida* for her to have been renamed, sailed to New Orleans, refitted with a new "bottom" then sailed to Havana and then to Pensacola. Just because the time schedule would allow does not mean that it happened.

The documentation shown above appears conclusive that Captain Pickle's *West Florida* and Captain Rousseau's

---

[134] *New Orleans: Fact and Legends* by Raymond Joseph Martinez and Jack D. L. Holmes, page 71.

Galvestown, also known as the *Galvez*, was at Mobile. Therefore the *West Florida* was not the renamed *Galvestown*.[135] They were different vessels. The *Galvez* and the *Galvestown* were one and the same.

Conclusion

The standard histories covering Mobile's colonial past make no mention of the fact that the Continental Navy assisted Spanish general Galvez in the taking of Mobile from the British in 1780. The immediate effect for those living in West Florida, including Mobile, of those efforts was to substitute one colonial master for another. But the efforts of Oliver Pollock and William Pickles and others to secure the submission of parts of West Florida north of Lake Pontchartrain and to assist in the capture

---

[135] On April 30, 1789 George Washington was inaugurated as first president of the United States on the balcony of Federal Hall in New York City. When Washington arrived in New York harbor by boat on April 23 he received a 13 gun salute from the Spanish Brigantine *Galvestown* thought to have been the very same vessel on which General Galvez made his entrance into Pensacola harbor. Perhaps not, as there was a new construction or rebuild of a Spanish naval vessel in New Orleans or Cuba, of a vessel named *Galveztown* in 1785. *Descriptive Catalog of the Documents relating to the History of the United States and the Papeles Procedentes de Cuba deposited in the Archivo General de Indias at Seville* by Roscoe R. Hill, published by the Carnegie Institute of Washington, 1916, Washington D. C., page 531.

of Mobile provided some legitimacy to the claim of the revolting thirteen colonies to parts of West Florida after they secured their independence as the United States. By 1812 Spain gave in to the inevitable and Colonial Mobile and West Florida was no more.

The decisive West Florida victory's by Bernardo de Galvez and his French and American allies in a far-flung outpost of the Spanish Empire made him a legitimate Spanish military hero. Captain William Pickles single ship victory over a British naval vessel with superior firepower on a lake far removed from the thirteen colonies struggle to throw off their British colonial masters and create a new nation brought no glory or recognition to Captain Pickles or to his sponsor Oliver Pollock. But Pollock, Pickles and the sloop *West Florida* are Mobile's direct connection to the Revolutionary War.

The story of the Continental Navy at Mobile deserved to be told. I hope you enjoyed the telling.

Index

13th Regiment of foot of the Virginia Continental Line, 18
16th infantry Regiment, 14
22nd infantry Regiment, 11
60th regiment, 12, 98
Active, HMS frigate, 51, 60
Alfred, USS, 15
Amite River, 24, 42, 114, 115, 116,120
Astilleros Nereo, 111, 121
Baton Rouge, 11, 85, 130
Beerman, Eric, 124
British West Florida, 6, 39, 60, 67
Brownhall, HMS, 91
Burden, Lieutenant George, 53, 57
Cabot, USS, 16
Caindre, 63, 65, 67, 70, 74, 78, 80, 81, 82, 83, 84, 127
Calvert, Capt. Joseph, 16, 24, 102
Campbell, Maj. Gen. John, 27, 42, 45, 46, 63, 68, 97, 97, 102
Carlisle, Pennsylvania, 29
Carteret, packet, 45
Chance, brig, 7, 51
Chapelle, Howard I., 54, 104, 110

Chester, Governor Peter, 45, 50, 55
Choctaw Point, 96, 102
Choctaws, 19
Clark, Gen. George Rogers, 19, 25, 31, 50
Clarke, Lt. Arthur, 68
Clinton, Gen. Sir Henry, 42, 59, 99
Coker, Hazel, 85, 90, 93
Coker, William S., 87, 90, 93, 124
Columbus, USS, 15
Comet, packet, 68
Comte de Maurepas, merchant vessel, 61
Cox, Capt. John, 33
De Koven, Mrs. Reagan, 16
Deer Point, 61, 69
Delaney, Caldwell, 117
DeVoe, Thomas E., 48
Dickson, Lt. Col., 42, 44, 45
Diligence, HMS, 53, 67
Dispatch,Schooner, 24, 32
Dog River, 96, 102,103
Dudley, Dr. William, 117
Dyer, Dr. J. O., 1133
Earl of Bathurst,ordinance ship, 60, 67, 68, 92
East Florida, 11, 12, 99
Fabel, Robin A., 32, 51

Farmar, Major Robert, 61, 128
Flectas, Domingo, 129
Florida, survey schooner, 51, 57
Fort Charlotte, 11, 95, 96, 102, 138
Fort Conde, 95
Fort Morgan, 82, 116
Fort Pitt, 17, 18, 20, 31, 36, 59
Fort St. John, 56, 57, 71, 76, 84, 127
Frederick, John, 61
Galveston Texas, 112
Galvez Brig, 102,129,130
Galvez Town, 42, 45, 113
Galvez, Bernardo de, 7, 15, 21, 31, 34, 39, 42, 43, 45, 46, 49, 56, 63, 64, 73, 80, 90, 91, 96, 102, 129, 130, 131
Galvez, brig, 91,95,102
Galveztown brigantine, 111, 118,130, 131
Galveztown, Louisiana, 112
Gauld, George, 81, 94
Gayton, Vice Admiral Clark, 50, 82
Gen. Pickering, privateer, 60
Geoffigons, 87
Germain, Lord George, 42
Hamilton, Colonel Henry, 26
Hamilton, Peter Joseph, 7, 26,42, 91,92,93, 95, 98, 102,118
Hampden, USS, 15
Hanxleden, Colonel Henry, 97
Haynes, Robert V., 13, 24
Higginbotham, Jay, 74, 80, 117
HMS Active, 60
HMS Hermes, 82
HMS Hound, 60
HMS Mentor, 54, 58, 60, 123, 124
HMS Port Royal, 61
HMS Stork, 61, 67
Holmes, Jack D.L., 12, 24, 74, 95, 114, 120, 122, 126, 129
Houston Chronicle, 120, 122
Howard I. Chapelle, 41, 53, 54, 64, 109, 110
Humphries, Josiah, 106
Hupp, Olin L., 18, 26
Independent Company of Western Pennsylvania, 33
Jones, John Paul, 15, 16
Joseph, ship, 32
Kirkland, Lieutenant, 51, 58
Koulician, Kings brig, 90
Krupp, Louis, 98
Lafitte, Captain Paul, 24
Lake Pontchartrain, 6, 11, 24, 62,66,70, 76, 82, 130

Laurens, Henry, 106,107,108
Le Mair, Captain James, 35
Lee, William, 109
LeMontais, Captain, 67, 70, 76
letter of Marque, 19, 33
Lewis, schooner, 35
Lighthouse Museum of St. Augustine, 111
Loyalists or Tories, 14
Madrid Gazette, 128
Malaga, Spain, 111, 112, 118
Manchac, 11, 43, 44, 46, 55, 57, 62, 77,114,120,129
Marley, David F., 25
Martin, Francois-Xavier, 37, 39, 99
Martinez, Raymond J., 72, 95, 126, 129
McComb, David G., 113
McIntosh, Captain, 19
McIntyre, Lieutenant Thomas, 22, 33
Mentor, HMS, 60, 61, 124, 128
Mercury packet, 106
Miranda, Francisco De, 124
Mississippi River, 6, 10, 11, 15, 24, 27, 32, 39, 41, 57, 59, 73, 84, 90, 93
Mississippi sound, 6

Mobile, 2, 6, 7, 10, 11, 12, 86, 118, 122, 123, 137, 138
Montgomery, G.E., 33
Morgan, Dr. William J,, 116
Morison, Samuel Eliot, 16
Morris, USS, 34
Morris, Robert, 17, 25, 33, 34, 35, 41, 63, 65, 67, 71, 74, 84
Morris's Tender, 63, 64, 67
Natchez, 7, 11, 13, 15, 16, 19, 20, 21, 47, 85,99
New Orleans, 6, 15, 18, 19, 21, 22, 30, 33, 35, 56, 62, 71, 84, 90
New Providence, Bahamas, 35
Norton, brig, 36
O'Reilly, Don Alexander, 29, 30
Parker, Admiral Sir Peter, 50, 51, 60, 67, 70
Paullin, Charles Oscar, 16, 21, 34, 64, 104, 108, 116, 122,124
Peck, John, 106
Pennell, Joseph, 105
Pensacola, 11, 15, 25, 33, 39, 42, 50, 51, 53, 54, 55, 59, 60, 67, 70, 85, 90, 96, 102, 111, 120, 124, 128, 129, 130
Perdido River, 10, 91

Philadelphia, 34, 107, 122
Philbrick, Nathaniel, 14
Pickler's Florida, 101, 117, 128
Pickles, William captain, 6, 34, 35, 62, 64, 85, 86, 105 106, 116, 120, 130, 131
Pollock, Oliver, 15, 21, 26, 29, 33, 35, 41, 62, 71, 77, 82, 88, 104, 130
Port Penn, 108
Port Vincent, 114
privateers, 7, 16, 32, 36
Providence, USS sloop, 15, 35
Provost, Colonel Augustine, 12
Rattletrap, keelboat, 16, 18, 19, 26, 59
Rea, Robert E., 94, 124
Rebecca, ship, 19, 22, 23, 25, 33, 34, 41, 64
Reprisal, privateer schooner, 24
Richtor, Henry, 37
Rillieux, Vincente, 24
Rousseau, Pierre George, 34, 63, 71, 72, 74, 79, 83, 94, 114, 120, 126, 129
Rowan, Captain, 35, 36
Royal Charlotte, brig, 30
Saratoga, US ship-rigged sloop, 108, 19
Savage, Jerrald, 71, 76, 77

Smithweck, David, 116
Solano, Jose, 124
South-Carolina and American General Gazette, 35
Spanish Louisiana, 6, 30, 31, 57
Spanish Replica, 111
St. Augustine Lighthouse and Museum, 112
Stephens, Philip, 57
Stork, HMS sloop, 51, 61, 67, 68, 70, 123
Sylph, sloop, 51, 123
Tensaw, 7, 11, 15, 26
Turner, Sam, 123
Urwin, Gregory J. W., 48
Venezuela, galliot, 89
Ventura, ship, 126, 129
Vestal, HMS, 109
Volante, frigate, 90, 93, 94
Waldecker Regiment, 24
Waldeckers, 27, 97
Ware, John D., 81
West Florida, vessel, 7, 45, 53, 63, 67, 70, 72, 76, 80, 83, 86, 104, 112, 115, 130
Who's Afraid, privateer, 60
Willing Raid, 17
Willing, James, 7, 16, 17, 19, 20, 21, 22, 23, 25, 26, 27, 31, 33, 35, 39, 51, 58, 59, 85

ABOUT THE AUTHOR

Sid Schell is a retired maritime lawyer living in Mobile, Alabama. Author of *Fort Powell and the Civil War Western Approaches to Mobile Bay 1861-1865*. For more than 40 years he has been building research files on Mobile and Southwest Alabama. He has written articles on the Civil War submarines and secret weapons tested at Mobile and on the forts at Oven and Choctaw Bluffs in Clark County, Alabama. A scuba diver, he has located and surveyed the Civil War vessels C.S.S. *Huntsville,* C.S.S. *Tuscaloosa and the* C.S.S. *Gaines.* Sidney served as a member of the Board of Directors of the History Museum of Mobile from the early 1980s with five terms as chairman. He was in 1985 appointed Adjunct Research Associate with the Department of Sociology/Anthropology with the University of South Alabama. He served on the Tecumseh commission, C.S.S. Alabama Commission and at one time chaired the Underwater Archaeology Committee for the Alabama Historic Commission. He is also an artist and ship model builder but primarily a grandfather trying to impart his love of history to his grandchildren Virginia, Sarah Frances and George.

Partially reconstructed Fort Conde/Charlotte in downtown Mobile, Alabama now a museum and welcome center operated by the History Museum of Mobile.

Printed in Great Britain
by Amazon